KU-144-560

UNIVERSITY OF
WINCHESTER

KA 0024831 2

# LANGUAGE AND LANGUAGE LEARNING

*General Editors:* RONALD MACKIN *and* PETER STREVENS

*Oxford University Press, Ely House, London W.1*

GLASGOW NEW YORK TORONTO MELBOURNE WELLINGTON
CAPE TOWN SALISBURY IBADAN NAIROBI DAR ES SALAAM LUSAKA
ADDIS ABABA BOMBAY CALCUTTA MADRAS KARACHI LAHORE DACCA
KUALA LUMPUR SINGAPORE HONG KONG TOKYO

*Paperback edition* ISBN 0 19 437045 3
*Library edition* ISBN 0 19 437116 6

© *Oxford University Press, 1971*

PRINTED IN GREAT BRITAIN BY HEADLEY BROTHERS LTD
109 KINGSWAY LONDON WC2 AND ASHFORD KENT

# The Social Meaning of Language

*J. B. PRIDE*

London

*OXFORD UNIVERSITY PRESS*

1971

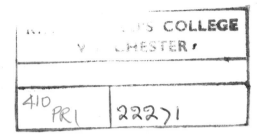

.....'S COLLEGE
.....HESTER,

410
PRI    22271

# Contents

# Introduction: Linguistics as a Social Science

The study of language as part of culture and society is a task that defies neat delimitation. One need only note, for example, how some of the more impressive bibliographies in this general area (for which we shall accept the common term 'socio-linguistics') show, relatively speaking, so few items in common with each other. D. H. Hymes's Reader bearing the title *Language in Culture and Society* refers to over two thousand different items—books, articles, reviews, and so on. But these are by no means duplicated by the seven hundred-odd items in the only slightly more recent *Selected Titles in Sociolinguistics* distributed by the Center for Applied Linguistics (Washington, D.C.). Moreover, neither of these overlaps very much with the 658 references built into the text of U. Weinreich's *Languages in Contact*, which in turn covers rather different ground, bibliographically as in other respects, from E. Haugen's equally comprehensive and valuable *Bilingualism in the Americas*. One could go on.

The reason for this state of affairs is, not unnaturally, that most, if not all, of the 'social sciences' are involved: notably psychology, social psychology, sociology, social anthropology, and anthropology; involved, too, at all descriptive and theoretical levels, not only directly but very often in passing. What is surprising is the relatively small extent to which *linguistics* has so far been concerned. The layman might (with some justification) suppose that linguistics had always provided at the very least a natural forum for discussion. He could scarcely, however, be more wrong. In many respects the position today is still aptly reflected in some words written in 1929 by E. Sapir: 'It is peculiarly important', he remarks, 'that linguists, who are often accused, and accused justly, of failure to look beyond the pretty patterns of their subject matter, should become aware of what their science may mean for the interpretation of human conduct in general. Whether they like it or not, they must become increasingly concerned with the many anthropological, sociological, and psychological problems which invade the field of linguistics' (E. Sapir, 1929). The essay itself was significantly titled 'The Status of Linguistics as a Science': significantly because the impetus to make linguistics a 'science' has since contributed in no small measure to notions of its relative independence from most of the other 'social sciences' (see for example N. Chomsky, 1965, p. 20). It cannot, it is true, now be said that linguistics continues to repel psychological problems, yet even so most linguists today are not sufficiently aware of, or concerned about, issues which encroach upon anthropology and sociology. This is the more surprising if one reflects that the first mainsprings of modern linguistics lay to a large extent in the work of anthropologists like F. Boas and E. Sapir.

For Sapir, whose insights are not to be taken lightly, the subject should be regarded as, above all, a *social* science. Much more recently R. A. Hall, Jr. (1965) has been moved to place a similar emphasis on the social character of language: '. . . there is the ever-present danger that . . . ultra-structured grammar will lose touch with linguistic reality, which is that of individual humans speaking to and responding to the speech of other individual humans in the context of their social relationships' (p. 345). Compare, too, C. A. Ferguson (1959): 'Descriptive linguists in their understandable zeal to describe the internal structure of the language they are studying often fail to provide even the most elementary data about the socio-cultural setting in which the language functions' (p. 437).

The most convincing developments in linguistics (as in other sciences) have usually been accompanied by re-evaluations not so much of method as of subject matter. Transformative-generative linguists have persuasively argued that scientific method is more properly the methods of sciences; that is to say, *each* science develops a large part of its method out of its subject matter; method is thus ultimately secondary. The aim of the present account will be to signpost some particular areas of this now rapidly expanding field (the most recent references incorporated in the present account are dated 1967).

## BIBLIOGRAPHIES, HISTORICAL SURVEYS, ETC.

'Bulletin Signaletique.' Section on 'Sociology of Language', in *Language Sciences*. Paris: Centre Nationale de la Recherche Scientifique. Quarterly.

COHEN, M. (1956). *Pour une Sociologie du Langage*. Paris: Albin Michel.

DEUTSCH, K. W. (1953). *Nationalism and Social Communication*. New York: John Wiley & Sons.

GOODELL, R. J. (1964). 'An ethnolinguistic bibliography with supporting material in linguistics and anthropology', in *Anthropological Linguistics*, 6, 2.

GUMPERZ, J. J. (1965b). 'Language', in *Biennial Review of Anthropology*, ed. Siegel, B. J. Stanford University Press.

HALL, R. A. (1966). *Pidgin and Creole Languages*. Cornell University Press.

HAUGEN, E. (1956). *Bilingualism in the Americas: A Bibliography and Research Guide*. American Dialect Society.

HOIJER, H. (1961). 'Anthropological linguistics', in *Trends in European and American Linguistics, 1936-1960*. Utrecht and Antwerp: Spectrum.

HYMES, D. H. (1963). 'Toward a history of linguistic anthropology', in *Anthropological Linguistics*, 5, 1.

HYMES, D. H. (1964a). 'Toward ethnographies of communication', in *American Anthropologist*, 66, 6, 2.

HYMES, D. H. (1964b). 'Directions in (ethno-) linguistic theory', in *American Anthropologist*, 66, 3, 2.

HYMES, D. H. (1964c). *Language in Culture and Society: A Reader in Linguistics and Anthropology*. Harper & Row.

International Bibliography of Social and Cultural Anthropology. London: Stevens & Sons Ltd.

International Bibliography of Sociology. London: Stevens & Sons Ltd.

Linguistic Bibliography. Permanent International Committee of Linguists. Utrecht: Spectrum.

Linguistic Reporter. Newsletter of the Centre for Applied Linguistics, 1717 Massachusetts Avenue, N.W. Washington, D.C. 20036.

LOUNSBURY, F. (1959, 1962). 'Language', in Siegel, B. J. (ed.) *Biennial Review of Anthropology*. Stanford University Press.

MOHRMANN, C. *et al.* (1961). *Trends in European and American Linguistics 1930–1960*. Utrecht and Antwerp: Spectrum.

PIKE, K. L. (1954–60). *Language in Relation to a Unified Theory of Human Behaviour*, Parts 1–3. Glendale, California, Summer Institute of Linguists.

STERN, H. H. (1962). *Foreign Languages in Primary Education*. UNESCO Institute for Education, Hamburg and OUP, London.

VILDOMEC, V. (1963). *Multilingualism*. A. W. Sythoff-Leyden.

WEINREICH, U. (1953). *Languages in Contact*. Mouton.

# 2 Language as Social Process

Socio-linguistics concerns itself with a range of problems extending all the way from the face-to-face 'encounter' or 'speech event' to the larger 'speech community'. The speech community as a field of study has attracted very much more attention than the speech event. It is, however, both an ambiguous and a complex term. It is ambiguous because it is often used both in the linguistic sense of 'a group of people who use the same system of speech signals' (L. Bloomfield, 1933, p. 29), and in the more sociological or anthropological sense in which the 'group of people' is defined socially as well as (or instead of) linguistically. In the former sense the focus is on one given language and its regional and social distribution; attention may also be given to the manner of its contact with other languages, and the corresponding contacts of their respective users (E. Haugen, 1953). Descriptive linguistic analysis may also extend to varieties of the language in question, and the presence or absence of such varieties may be correlated with social factors.

Community-centred studies on the other hand are concerned with how a given speech community draws selectively upon two or more languages, dialects, or language varieties. An obvious problem here is the extent to which the community in question is identified on linguistic as well as on social grounds.

The most self-evident socially defined group of people is the nation or state itself. H. Kloss (1966), for example, equates 'community' with 'state' without comment, and goes on to characterize states in terms of mono-, bi-, and multi-lingualism. C. A. Ferguson (1962a), W. A. Stewart (1962a), and several other scholars accept the nation as their natural basic unit. U. Weinreich (1953, p. 83 ff.; 1957, esp. p. 203 ff.) displays a pronounced bias towards national groupings in speaking of 'bilingual communities' and 'language contact situations', but at the same time is even more concerned with 'mother-tongue groups'. This last term is stated to be less 'ambiguous' than 'speech community' for the investigation of bilingualism, the discovery of who learns whose language (see esp. 1957), how 'reported' mother-tongue groupings differ from 'observed', and so forth.

J. J. Gumperz (1962b, p. 31) on the other hand sees the 'linguistic community' as 'a social group . . . held together by the frequency of social interaction patterns and set off from the surrounding area by weaknesses in the lines of communication'. This is a definition which more easily allows variation in scale from large community right down to small group, and is not intended to exclude the possibility of areal overlappings of communities. Perhaps not everyone would wish to recognize the criterial importance of *frequency* of interaction (which might seem to favour a fundamentally sociological bias), but even so (as a brief statement of a complex notion) it typifies a dominant perspective in present-day socio-linguistics. On the one hand the main focus rests not on language but on social group, which at the same time is itself identified—at least in part—by its linguistic attributes (i.e. it is not *necessarily* a nation, or a socio-economic class, or an age-group, etc.). Its make-up is thus problematical; so problematical in fact that D. H. Hymes (1964c, p. 386) for one is tempted to express the need to develop a 'new, second, qualitative and descriptive science of language, beside that of the linguistic code per se'.

The study of speech communities offers a large number of points of departure. We shall start (it may be quite arbitrarily) with the use and development of the term 'domain'. Domains of language use have been described as 'the occasions on which one language (variant, dialect, style, etc.) is habitually employed rather than (or in addition to) another' (J. A. Fishman, 1966, p. 428). Recurrent domains would be such as 'the family', 'the neighbourhood', 'governmental administration', 'occupations', and so forth. The overall pattern of description is that of the 'dominance configuration' of a speech community, which can be expressed diagrammatically: 'domains of language behaviour' horizontally and 'other sources of variance' (written/

spoken medium, 'formal'/'informal' style, 'production'/'reception'/'inner speech') vertically, each intersection marked for choice (and directions of change in choice) of language. Some domains will be shown to be more, and some less, 'maintenance-prone' in the given language contact setting than others.

The term 'dominance configuration' was first used by U. Weinreich, in his very valuable *Languages in Contact* (1953). In Weinreich's view each one of a bilingual's languages may be 'dominant' (or not dominant) in terms of several criteria: relative proficiency, mode of use, order of learning and age, usefulness in communication, emotional involvement, function in social advance, and literary-cultural value. Each is discussed in turn (p. 75–9). The specific question of 'domains' is treated under the heading of 'functions' (p. 87, 88). It is difficult, however, to estimate Weinreich's view of the relative importance of domain. On p. 98 it is stated that the 'difficulty of ranking two mother-tongue groups in hierarchical order is aggravated by the need to rank functions of the languages as well'. He goes on (p. 98) to elevate 'differences in social status' above functional diversity as an 'expedient' restriction of the term 'dominant'. However, further on, and now in connection with 'language shifts', it is stated that these 'should be analysed in terms of the functions of the languages in the contact situation, since a mother-tongue group may switch to a new language in certain functions but not in others' (p. 107). At this point, reference is made to the discussion of domains on p. 87. Also at this point Weinreich interestingly enough relegates 'a simple statement as to which language has higher "prestige" or "social value" ' to a lesser place behind domain analysis and analysis of such matters as urbanization, religious affiliation, and so forth (p. 108).

In effect Fishman clarifies certain developing tendencies observable in Weinreich's work. He particularly stresses that 'the appropriate designation and definition of domains of language behaviour . . . calls for considerable insight into the socio-cultural dynamics of particular multilingual settings at particular periods in their history'; further, that 'since we are concerned with the possibility of stability or change in language behaviour on the one hand, we must be equally concerned with all of the forces contributing to stability or to change in human behaviour more generally, on the other' (p. 441). There is need for 'more general theories of personal, social and cultural change . . . it will be necessary for the study of language maintenance and language shift to be conducted within the context of studies of intergroup contacts that attend to important other-than-language processes: urbanization (ruralization) industrialization (or its abandonment), nationalism (or de-ethnization) . . .', etc. The overall objective is a 'typology of language contact situations' (p. 446) capable of systematizing how, for example, the 'American immigrant case' differs from the 'Anglo-American conquest case', and so on. He goes on to suggest that although 'anthropologists, historians, linguists, sociologists and psychologists' have long studied 'phenomena related to language maintenance and language shift', yet 'only rarely and recently has such interest led to a definition and formulation of this field of study in its own right' (fn. 2, p. 424).

Elsewhere (1965), Fishman distinguishes another type of domain, this time defined in terms of 'stylistic level'. One now takes into consideration, as primary defining characteristics, scales of inter-personal and inter-group relationship such as intimacy—distance, formality—informality, solidarity—non-solidarity, status, power, etc. Both types of domain can be differentiated into (linguistically relevant) 'role relations', such as judge-petitioner, shopkeeper-customer, husband-wife, etc. The real question is, however, whether to accept the first or the second type of domain as nearest the heart of the matter, whether, for instance, to see role relations largely in terms of stylistic level or largely in terms of more physically defined settings— accepting all these expressions rather loosely for the moment. Fishman himself quite briefly dismisses the former, mainly on the grounds that it cannot easily be empirically investigated. But there seems every reason to believe that whatever may be the more methodologically expedient the real subject matter which we are seeking has a great deal more to do, ultimately, with *relationships* of this other sort.

J. J. Gumperz (1965a) and J.-P. Blom and J. J. Gumperz (1967) stand somewhat closer to this point of view. Gumperz uses a slightly different terminology ('social relationship' for 'role relationship'), but the important point to note is that main emphasis is placed on the social anthropologist's concept of 'status' in defining such relationships: status that is to say seen in terms of positions—rights and duties assigned by the culture—occupied within the social system. This sort of emphasis is absent, or at any rate not made explicitly, in Fishman's account (1966, p. 431). At the same time, there is a close correspondence between Gumperz' 'social occasion' ('more or less closely defined behavioural routines which are kept separate by members of a society', 1965a), and Fishman's view of domain.

Gumperz considers both social relationships and (it would seem) social occasions to be finite in number for any given society (1965a, p. 84; 1964, p. 139). The question of finiteness is clearly of some importance, and prompts interest in anthropological approaches to 'status' relationships like that of W. H. Goodenough (1965). Goodenough makes a clear distinction between composite identities assumed by a person (along with identity relationships) on the one hand, and component statuses which enter into and define these on the other. Depending on the 'occasion', so a given individual selects particular identities in which to present himself to the world. Statuses, identities, and identity relationships he thinks are quite limited in number for any given society, yet at the same time co-occur in an (analogously speaking) 'grammatical' manner (p. 7). How they do this constitutes the overall 'system' of social relations. Statuses themselves are rights and duties expressed as deference, cordiality, reverence, affection, sexual distance, emotional independence, etc. In cases of incompatibility among any of these, various adjustments are made: one or more may be dropped or replaced, or some form of 'conditioned variant' selected, rather as in the case of phonetic assimilation (p. 22, fn. 14). Not only is it likely, in Goodenough's view, that all such relationships are indeed limited in number, but also that each particular status scale may call for no more than seven 'discriminations' in our handling of them—this mainly in view of psychological evidence concerning human brain capacities: see for example G. A. Miller's well-known article of 1956. Goodenough concludes, however, that if many status dimensions are involved, it may still be a cumbersome and difficult task to handle them all.

It is instructive to relate non-linguistic theoretical discussions of this sort not only to domain analysis but also to such ostensibly linguistic constructs as, for example, the 'scale of formality'; the use of precisely five cardinal points ('frozen'—'consultative'—'casual'—'familiar'—'intimate') may be felt in this way to gain validity (see M. Joos, 1962). Equally fundamental, however, is the processual question of *how* people interact on particular occasions in selecting, replacing, or modifying statuses. This is the theme of a rewarding set of three lectures by F. Barth (1966) entitled *Models of Social Organization*. Barth is not impressed by the endeavour to describe the surface regularities of social form, nor even to provide a static description of cultural constraints and incentives (or 'values') that lie behind these. His concern is instead with the structure of processes of interaction which reflect such constraints and incentives and themselves '*generate*' formal patterns. In simple terms 'participants' engage in 'skewed communication', over- and under-communicating statuses felt or desired to belong to the occasion. The cumulative effect of such processes is that of institutionalization, or the development of conventional behaviours in which statuses co-occur in some regular fashion; but their on-going nature is that of reciprocal 'transactions' (in a sense bargains) in which participants 'try to assure that the value gained for them is greater or equal to the value lost' (p. 4). The process itself, in Barth's opinion, is *observable*. Quite liberal examples are provided (p. 6 ff., p. 16 ff., etc.).

In this light culture is not seen as some kind of static 'integrated' whole (rather as one might see language as fully integrated langue), and 'incapable of empirical investigation'. Instead, 'values are empirical facts which may be discovered' (p. 12), because ultimately subject to observable transactional processes. Such processes (*a*) create consistency among values (in the sense that values of different orders may have to be reconciled on any given occasion) and (*b*) resolve 'dilemmas of choice' by the construction of 'over-arching principles of evaluation' that in turn feed back into and modify prior systems of values. Barth places considerable weight on such feed-back effects, stressing their origin in real (and possibly novel) transactional situations. In short, 'action' has 'developmental primacy over institutionalized value' (p. 16). Without action, the argument goes on, consistency in values is not attained.

Barth's view of social form as fundamentally processual and subject to empirical study is challenging and relevant. It allows, as any theory of human behaviour must, for what Dorothy Lee calls 'autonomous motivation'. Different academic disciplines are likely to reach the same conclusion; biologically, for example, 'The organism should not be considered as a responding machine but rather as primary activity' (D. Lee, 1961, p. 110). Linguistic activity is best regarded as in large measure autonomously motivated transactional behaviour capable of symbolizing, reinforcing and modifying value systems.

But what are some of the values, or constraints and incentives, that enter into linguistically mediated transactions? One is at once up against the problems of terminology and generality. It is not too difficult to provide evidence showing just how dangerous generalizations such as group intactness, class, prestige, etc., can be (see, for example, J. A. Fishman, 1966, p. 442 ff.). One can readily agree with the view that 'We very much need a more refined understanding of the circumstances under which behaviours towards language and behaviours toward the group are related to each other in *particular* ways' (p. 443). Yet, at the same time, investigation of how choice of language symbolizes and alters values is still essential. We shall therefore go on to refer to some aspects of current socio-linguistic work which seem on the face of it to bear upon these matters.

# 3   Social Values of Language

The British sociologist, B. Bernstein, discusses choice of variety (or 'code') of English in relation to activities and relationships which on the one hand stress 'loyalty to the group' and 'insulate the speaker from personal involvement', and on the other stress the expression of individual meaning and allow an 'acquisition of skills which are strategic for educational and occupational success'. Part of Bernstein's hypothesis (1966 is a recently published statement) is, or has been, that the distinction between 'some sections of the working class strata, especially lower working class', and, in contrast, 'middle class and associated strata', is matched very closely with the distinction between the availability (for the lower working class) of a group-oriented 'restricted' code of English, and, for the rest of the population, the availability of this code *plus* an individual-oriented 'elaborated' code.

One of his less familiar examples (1964) is that of the middle-class psychiatrist who poses an unfamiliar problem for his working-class patient, that of elaborating his own personality. Then again, to take quite another kind of example, J. Klein (1965)—who refers to Bernstein's work a great deal—sees the same factors at work in some husband-wife quarrels, where 'problems will be phrased in an incomplete way and the real nature of the decision may never be revealed' (p. 173). Klein speaks of the 'cognitive poverty' of certain sectors in society, which she calls a 'stubborn determination not to develop' (p. 87): that is to say, in large part a disinclination to develop the power to express *oneself*.

But of course it is especially in the younger formative years that verbal skills are channelled into their various courses, and it is on these earlier stages that Bernstein's work mainly bears.

We shall return later to this matter, but not without first noting one or two of the more clearly problematical aspects of his general position.

In various places Bernstein provides structural details of the two codes. The restricted code, for example, is said to be very much the more predictable in every respect, characteristically displaying short and often unfinished and grammatically simple sentences, active voice, little use of subordinate clauses, limited use of adjectives and adverbs and conjunctions, and so forth. It serves, and in these respects may perhaps serve well, 'to increase consensus'. One is liable to be struck, however, not only by the 'restricted' nature (in many criterial respects) of much serious educated discussion, but also by a puzzling distinction (made as recently as 1966) between 'linguistic' and 'verbal' on the one hand and 'paralinguistic' and 'extraverbal' on the other. Grammatical and lexical contrast are seen to belong with the first, while factors of rhythm, stress, pitch, etc., are regarded (along with gesture and facial expression) as aspects of the second. The elaborated and restricted codes are said to lean heavily in the one and the other direction respectively. In the former, 'meanings will have to be expanded and raised to the level of *verbal* explicitness', while in the latter 'the unique meaning of the individual is likely to be verbally implicit'. One would rather imagine, however, that a fairly crucial ability in the cultured person is that of handling a large range of inter-personal meanings through the use of systematically contrasted features of intonation and so forth—these being just as much *linguistic* as paralinguistic or extralinguistic. But even if this were not so, it is misleading to convey the impression that the use by the restricted code user of phonological resources in the language is in any sense not linguistic.

Bernstein's view of language as primarily or largely an instrument for the expression or suspension of individuality might seem at first sight to correspond closely to Gumperz's distinction between (respectively) individualizing or 'personal' and non-individualizing or 'transactional' settings (J. J. Gumperz, 1966).

In his account of 'code-switching' between 'rana målet' (the local dialect) and 'bokmål' (the literary, religious, and generally high prestige dialect), in a Norwegian country district, Gumperz refers to various 'social networks' (religious, political, and so forth), but quickly dispenses with these in favour of a specific set of distinctions. These are: between 'closed' and 'open' friendship groups (rather in the manner of the sociological distinction between 'primary' and 'secondary' groups: see W. J. H. Sprott, 1958; also W. W. and W. E. Lambert, 1964, p. 87 ff.), between 'personal' and 'transactional' settings, and between local and non-local topics. Choice of dialect is related therefore to what amounts to eight possible combinations of these factors:

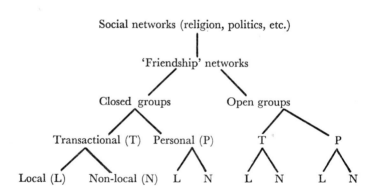

Although both Bernstein and Gumperz handle a basically individualizing/non-individualizing contrast, the terms themselves are far from equivalent; what happens in Norway—which is to say among Gumperz's subjects—seems (as it is described) to be so different from what happens among Bernstein's subjects that the similarity in terms is clearly in need of a good deal of qualification. The 'transactional' or non-individualizing setting attracts the high-status 'bokmål', the language of etiquette, regardless of whether the network happens to be open or closed; for Bernstein, on the other hand, suspension of individuality is achieved through the use of a 'restricted' code, which is in no obvious way comparable with 'bokmål'. The 'personal' or individualizing setting in Norway on the other hand attracts the more familiar and relaxed rural dialect, but for Bernstein the sense of 'personal' connotes the use of an 'elaborated' code; and again there is no obvious equivalence. Conversely, the non-personal 'bokmål' (or 'bokmål' in its non-personal forms) would seem to relate most nearly to an educated but (on occasion) ritualized *restricted* code—the use of which is one of several necessary qualifications to Bernstein's position.

In a more recent treatment of code-switching in the same locality, J.-P. Blom and J. J. Gumperz (1967) move closer to Bernstein in remarking on the linguistic habits of a group of (middle-class) students who had been away at university: they are observed to switch codes in immediate response to particular *topics*, switching, that is to say, between the local dialect and a 'mixed' form of speech that incorporates features of the standard language. Switching of this sort symbolizes shifts in cultural identities and social values, 'allegiances', and so forth. One might recognize here some reflection of middle-class verbal behaviour as seen by Bernstein, in the sense that statuses can be signalled as relevant or not relevant to the occasion by shift of language.

The difficulty in determining just how far any two approaches are or are not comparable crops up continually. W. A. Stewart (1962c), in dealing with choice by the individual of French or Creole in Haiti, states that: 'two main kinds of behavioural variables play an important role as the determiners of language usage in any social situation'; these are, namely, whether the occasion is private or public, and whether the relationship is 'formalized' or 'unformalized':

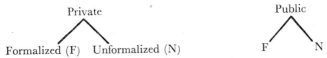

Private                                        Public

Formalized (F)   Unformalized (N)         F        N

A formalized relationship is said to be one which gives rise to highly predictable and normative language. This of course is a prime characteristic of Bernstein's restricted code. An unformalized relationship is what one finds in 'informal gatherings' (rather than in 'official ceremonies' and the like). But the informal gathering is just the kind of setting that might (here as elsewhere, presumably) trigger off and be sustained by, again, some form of restricted code. The link with Bernstein is once more rather tenuous, if only in the sense that more might be said about the meanings of terms like 'formalized'.

The meaning of the notion 'formality', like that of 'prestige', is particularly elusive. It is very widely used in connection with choice of language, not least in linguistics. To the linguist participant (or role) relationships are not so much regarded as naturally reducible to some single non-linguistic scale of formality as describable *linguistically* in these terms. This being the case, it is likely that what the linguist means and what, say, the social psychologist means by formality may be two distinct things, further differentiated on the linguistic side in accordance with the various theories of grammar (etc.) underlying description. There is a useful though brief discussion of formality in J. L. Fischer (1958). Fischer questions whether there might or might not be a more or less universal 'formality complex' to which many diverse factors contribute: compliance, tenseness, femaleness, topic, socio-economic class, etc. But whether this is so or not he is surely right to suggest that in different cultures the 'same' inter-personal factors may not co-occur to constrain choice of linguistic form upon any *one* such scale. At the same time, this is a relative matter, and if different languages do appear to express 'formality complexes', which in some senses are comparable in spite of their diverse linguistic expression, then this is a *linguistic* fact of some importance. Also of some importance are the evident ways in which language helps (or seems to help) to reduce these, like other complexities, to fewer or more simple dimensions. Take, for example, the very largely morphological marking in the Bantu language Yao of what might otherwise appear to be a rather heterogeneous set of role relationships. The single (perhaps arbitrary) term 'formality' can be applied to these partly or perhaps largely at the prompting of the language (K. Mbaga and W. H. Whiteley, 1961; compare, too, the discussion above of W. Goodenough, 1965).

Here, as in the case of the notion 'speech community', and indeed in all areas of socio-linguistics, definition can neither attain complete precision nor be entirely linguistic—in accepted senses of the term. Another example is that of prestige. J. L. Fischer (1958, p. 486 ff.) expresses a fairly commonly held view: '. . . people adopt a variant primarily . . . because it expresses how they feel about their relative status versus other conversants', thus bringing about a 'protracted pursuit of an élite by an envious mass and consequent flight of the élite', this being 'the most important mechanism in linguistic drift'. He goes on to discuss the need to apply prestige indices to linguistic variants—indices whose 'threshold' will fall as time goes on (necessitating the appearance of new series of variants, to be chased in turn . . .). Fischer admits, however, that an élite is not to be easily identified, and adds: 'The study of social factors in linguistic drift is in the field of the sociology of language rather than linguistics proper.' U. Weinreich (1957) makes much the same point: 'The linguist's oversimplified model of a "prestige slope" on which innovations slide down will presumably be modified to allow for the diffusion of foreign material into national languages in a slangy "anti-prestige" direction' (p. 191). D. Hymes (1961b) writes that a language may be retained without its possessing prestige, as, for example, in the case of 'anti-white language loyalty' (p. 62 ff.). He warns the reader, therefore, to beware of 'the blanket term of an unanalysed differential "prestige"' (p. 74).

There is an interesting brief discussion in S. Silverman (1966, p. 917 ff.) of what 'power' and 'prestige' are. In particular he points out that 'social intimacy' is not always expressive of 'social equality'—in the sense of equality of prestige. Nor will socio-economic rank, education, or any other census item necessarily correspond with prestige as responded to by the bearers of the culture concerned. 'Prestige' (like 'formality', 'power', 'solidarity', and the like) is a many-faceted notion which demands of the linguist that he be something else besides in order the more validly to make certain types of linguistic statement. Nor should it be forgotten that the validity of all such general factors, even when all agree about their relevance to choice of language, depends partly on precise situational circumstances. F. W. Householder (1962) provides some interesting details concerning the uses of the 'literary standard' Katharevusa (K) and 'dialectal' Demotic (D) in present-day Greece. The mere recognition of the former as the literary standard does not in itself, for example, predict the equal representation D in the literature of art history, biography, and some scientific writing; nor the exclusive use of it in most newspapers for news stories as well as for editorials; nor its use for 'social' letters; nor its inappropriateness for nearly all artistic, literary, and theatre criticism; and so forth.

A currently favoured contrast in socio-linguistics is that between 'power' and 'solidarity' as determinants of verbal behaviour (see esp. R. Brown and A. Gilman, 1960). 'Power' may be no easier to define than 'prestige': Douglas Jay, one-time President of the Board of Trade, once made the whimsical remark that 'power is rather a myth, a very difficult animal to find once you're in contact with it'. In a sense, any functional attribute of a language confers 'power' on the user. The 'high' variety in a situation of diglossia, if indeed it 'is not used by any sector of the community for ordinary conversation' (C. A. Ferguson, 1959, p. 435), must correspondingly lack power of a certain sort— the fate of Sanskrit and Latin in particular among high-status literary languages needs no more than mere mention.

Casual conversational language and vernacular languages, each have a special kind of power, contributing to and deriving from the strength of small-group solidarity. One recalls the well-known passage by E. Sapir (1931a): 'Generally speaking, the smaller the circle, and the more complex the understanding already arrived at within it, the more economical can the act of communication afford to become. A single word passed between members of an intimate group, in spite of its apparent vagueness and ambiguity, may constitute a far more precise communication than volumes of carefully prepared correspondence interchanged between two governments.' There is reason to take what Sapir is saying here quite literally, not so much in order to advocate the promotion of local vernaculars at the expense of more widespread languages, as to retain regard for the unique effectiveness of many languages or dialects precisely because they serve this purpose so well. If a 'restricted code' exists for English it, too, has power (and, incidentally, aesthetic qualities, hence a kind of status: see B. Bernstein, 1961a, p. 308; and A. A. Hill, 1958, p. 291), the power which comes from social cohesiveness and feelings of identity, the power the politician and advertiser alike seek to tap. Paraguay has been called an interesting 'language laboratory' in that it presents a picture of unusually stable co-existence between a world language, Spanish, and a geographically restricted vernacular, Guarani. J. Rubin (1962) points out that (at the time of writing) 52 per cent of the population were bilingual in these languages. Spanish is the language of 'power', Guarani of 'solidarity', broadly speaking. Rubin wishes to explain choice of one or the other in terms of this pair of axes first, and others (socio-economic class, urban/rural origin, topic, sex, etc.) second. The interesting (and in a sense powerful) slot is where positive solidarity intersects with equality of prestige. Here Guarani is the normal medium.

But it is difficult to generalize, except again in terms of 'dilemmas of choice' in which some form of value equilibrium is sought. The predicament of the Hawaiian schoolchild faced with the uncomfortable problem of having to code-switch on appropriate occasions between the high-prestige standard English he is taught at school and the form of 'vulgar' English (related historically to pidgin English) which far more effectively symbolizes solidarity with his peers (*Anthropological Linguistics*, 6, 7, Oct. 1964, p. 76 ff.)—and for this reason possesses, for him, prestige of its kind—can be illustrated all over the world in many different contexts. Some form of shift in value equilibrium will account, for example, for the phenomenon of 'age-grading' whereby a low prestige dialect is consistently used among lower class Negro boys (rather than girls) in Washington D.C. who have not yet been 'acculturated' to the more prestigious dialect (W. A. Stewart, 1964). At the age of 7 or 8, noticeable dialect shifting takes place, fairly independently (in Stewart's view) of formal education.

The power of language or of a particular form of language to confer solidarity brings with it a very real, if often insecure, form of prestige. W. Labov (1963) relates the tendency to centralize diphthongs among inhabitants of Martha's Vineyard, a small island off Massachusetts, to feelings of resentment against incoming economic exploiters; fishermen in particular, and of a certain age (30–45), form the focal point for the expression (including linguistic expression) of independence. 'I think we use an entirely different type of English language' expresses consciousness of the need for prestige attaching to solidarity. 'Hypercorrection' is most pronounced among young men who had left for the mainland but then returned; and it may be noted in passing that hypercorrection may also be a normal feature of upward social mobility (Labov, 1966b), hence very much an expression of a need for prestige. U. Weinreich (1953) suggests that frustrated superiority feelings can give rise to intense language loyalty, resentment being caused 'among the more steadfast members of the dominated group, a resentment which brings with it unswerving language loyalty' (p. 101). However, as J. A. Fishman points out (1966, p. 444, 445), this would be a questionable generalization if taken too far, and Weinreich, too, concedes the need for qualification, in pointing out that 'a group's language loyalty and nationalistic aspirations do not necessarily have parallel goals' (p. 100).

Again in this broad connection of 'power' and 'solidarity' it should be remembered that choice or use of language is not unconnected with motivations for language learning. W. E. Lambert, R. C. Gardner, R. Olton and K. Tunstall (1961) report a large statistical study of, primarily, the effects of two types of motivation, which they term 'instrumental' and 'integrative', among high school pupils studying French in three localities in America. Integrative motivation is their main focus of interest, it being reasoned that 'the more utilitarian value of linguistic achievement, such as getting ahead in one's occupation' (instrumental motivation) might be 'appropriate for short-term goals . . . but lack the persistence quality which we assumed must be operative in the laborious task of acquiring a new language' (R. C. Gardner, 1966, p. 26). A close inspection of the original statistics, however, which include several differently angled measures of integrative motivation ('a subject's dissatisfaction or discouragement with his place in society', 'prejudiced orientations towards foreign peoples', 'personal preference for one's own culture' in terms of 'invidious comparisons', attitudes towards Franco-Americans, attitudes towards voices speaking French and English on tape, etc.), shows quite clearly that the learner's achievement seems to be relateable to these distinct types of motivation differently for different settings (see W. E. Lambert *et al.*, 1961, Part I, p. 33). In the Maine setting integrative motivation appears to be quite significant, but this cannot be said for Louisiana and Connecticut: evaluation reactions to people speaking French on tape, for example, may show sharp negative stereotypes yet not necessarily correlate in the least with any factor of linguistic achievement or aptitude. It is clearly no easier to generalize about language learning motivation in these terms than about motivations for language use.

Perhaps further illustration is necessary. For American students studying French in Louisiana and Connecticut the ('integrative') F-Scale and Orientation Index scores correlate very poorly with scores for 'oral production', 'achievement', and 'aptitude'. Each of these two indices were obtained from replies to questionnaires asking for reasons for studying French (Part I, p. 7, 8). Neither correlate at all impressively with 'intensity of motivation', with the exception of the Orientation Index in Connecticut. Correlation with 'ability to comprehend complex discussions in French' averages approximately nil (that is to say, there are negative correlations); it is of interest, however, to note that verbal I.Q. fares no better in this respect, whereas a seemingly semi-creative item on J. B. Carroll's battery of aptitude tests ('spelling clues') achieves some measure of significance. (There are notable differences in the Maine results, however, particularly with respect to the F-Scale Index, reflecting 'authoritative or undemocratic tendencies and generalized prejudicial orientations towards foreign peoples'.) Instrumental motivation ratings fare, on the whole, even worse than integrative ratings. At the same time, *intensity* of motivation (in terms of work done for assignments, future intentions to study and make use of the language, amount of practice given to the language, etc.) correlates reasonably well with 'mid-year French grades', etc.—as one might expect. So whence, one might ask, does the intensity arise? There seems little doubt that the socio-linguist interested in language learning motivation had best be interested in the *detailed* aspirations of the language user, rather than in anything so neat as precisely two types of motivation. Yet these seemingly quantifiable factors appeal widely. J. B. Carroll (1962), for example, refers to the same two types of motivation, and specifies each as positive, neutral, and negative.

The link between 'power' (and 'prestige' of a certain sort) as a factor governing choice of language and 'instrumental' motivation is obvious. So, too, is that between 'solidarity' (with the users of the other language) and 'integrative' motivation. The same broad distinction is reflected in the now commonly accepted opposition between the terms 'foreign language' (learned largely for the cultural insight it may provide) and 'second language' (learned largely for more utilitarian purposes: see P. Christophersen, 1960; and British Council, 1960–61). At the same time, however, it should be remembered that the other *language* will in any case, to varying extents, be responsive to the forms of the learner's own culture. And it must not be forgotten either that judicious selection of material to be learned—that is to say selection on socio-cultural as well as other grounds—can play a large part in achieving a *two-way* movement of cultural content. The other language in other words can be made to 'integrate' with the learner's own culture. The language-learning question at issue need not therefore amount to a cut-and-dried choice between exposure to the other culture ('solidarity' with it, 'integrative' motivation, 'foreign' language, etc.) on the one hand, and the use of the second language for utilitarian purposes ('power', 'instrumental' motivation, 'second' language, etc.) on the other. In many parts of the world a basic need is precisely that of expressing one's own culture linguistically through means other than one's native language.

The writer's experience of advising on the teaching of English at the State University of Ulan Bator, in the Mongolian People's Republic, and teaching English there, during April and May 1966, proved instructive in this respect. A run-down of some favourite learners' 'centres of interest' (requiring expression in English) might be interestingly compared with those which might obtain elsewhere: agriculture, especially animal husbandry, land cultivation, dairy farming, etc.; travel inside and outside the country, including transport by ox, camel, and horse; national customs and legends; sport, especially wrestling, horse-racing, and archery; Mongolian cooking; at home, especially the 'yurt' in the countryside; research into locally relevant scientific and technological problems; wild life and hunting; clothes, especially the national dress; sightseeing, especially museums of historical interest; and so on. These are not, of course, wholly unpredictable—as mere labels. But it is what English looks like in expressing each of these that is distinctive (for a brief example, see J. B. Pride, 1968). Moreover, it is only to a limited extent that the true nature and relevance of each centre of interest to the use of English can be properly assessed by making a survey of current practice, since in this as in many contexts English has a number of uses that are only *potential* until there are those competent to realize (indeed recognize) them.

Acceptance of a meaningful contrast between notions like power and solidarity is not disallowed merely because they tend on inspection to ramify in so many ways. Their application in socio-linguistics is likely to figure more and more as time goes on.

It may be worth mentioning therefore that social psychologists like M. Argyle (1967) accept the likelihood of two such major and partly independent dimensions of social motivation—which he happens to call dominance and affiliation—in non-linguistic as well as linguistic contexts. It may be worth noting, too, that at the sociological level Argyle defines 'social classes' in a rather analogous way, as 'groups of people who regard members of the other groups as inferior or superior, and where each group has a common culture' ('culture' is later explained as a function of 'common ideas and beliefs').

Underlying a good deal of what has been said so far is the very important distinction between bilingualism and biculturalism, either of which may occur without the other. The linguistic effects of the latter, even alone, can be considerable. Exposure to a new and attractive (or enviable, etc.) culture, without knowledge of its language, may result in the coining of new words and phrases and the extension of old meanings (although these processes need not result *only* from acculturation: T. E. Hope, 1962–3).

Relationships between bilingualism and biculturalism can be studied at various levels. A. R. Diebold (1962) examines, at the level of the community at large, ways in which 'culture change in rural Middle America is very much bound up with becoming bilingual in Spanish'. Social mobility in this part of the world depends to some considerable extent on the acquisition of and even shifting to Spanish. Diebold retook a village-wide census of one small Huave-speaking Mexican community, measuring proficiencies in Spanish alongside sex, age, occupation, etc. Spanish, the language used outside the community, is resisted within it owing to factors of endogamy, residence patterns, religious and political duties, and so forth. 'The only effective way to break these social bonds is to openly defect'; bilingualism and biculturalism are here in a state of near equilibrium. In contrast with Diebold's treatment of the subject there is that of N. A. McQuown (1962) also set in Mexico—this time at the level of the individual. The author subjects five Mexican bilingual informants (one Spanish-speaking non-Indian 'Ladino' and four vernacular-speaking Indians) to TAT and photographic 'cultural projection' tests, seeking to relate responses to these with linguistic admixtures of Spanish and Indian vernacular. Only two informants showed themselves to be both bilingual *and* markedly bicultural, in the sense that although, as in two cases, the native speaker of an Indian vernacular might display much evidence of 'hispanicising' and 'slavish literal translation' in his use of the vernacular, at the same time he would show very little sympathy or sense of identity with the Ladino culture. Further than this, there is an evident distinction between *knowledge of* and *feeling for* the other culture (McQuown's informant no. 4). This study is concerned to explore the characteristics of bilingual mediators between two cultures, bringing into consideration the interplay of social and personal values with choice of language.

# 4 Code-switching

The social value of language reveals itself in all manner of socially motivated verbal behaviour. Possibilities exist not only for seemingly straightforward and stable code-switching, but also for the lapse of one or other of the constituent codes and for the acceptance of another form of speech in partial or complete replacement. Then there is the possibility of borrowing items and features, either in an unassimilated form (Haugen's term 'integration' is useful for this) or in an assimilated form (which he calls 'interference'). All these behaviours can occur together or separately, and not only languages but also dialects and styles or varieties of language may be involved.

Code-switching between distinct languages is a normal activity in many parts of the world, some areas being especially marked for linguistic diversity: India for example—particularly Assam—the Caucasus, Mexico, New Guinea, parts of Nigeria, etc. (see U. Weinreich, 1957). One has always to take into account the distinction between, on the one hand, community (or national) and on the other individual bilingualism and multilingualism. The two are not necessarily closely related. One can find a large number of different inter-relationships between community and individual monolingualism, bilingualism, multilingualism, and diglossia. One should note that a community whose members possess one 'mother tongue' (or pre-school language) and many of whom go on to learn and use another language can be referred to as 'monolingual' *or* 'bilingual'; in applying these terms therefore one has to be careful to specify their meaning.

The need for qualification is evident again if one turns to Lambert's work in Canada. In this context, he suggests an 'instrumental'/'integrative' explanation for the fact that in Canada those who speak French are largely bilingual, whereas those who speak English are not: integrative motivation is seen as 'a psychological reaction to the contrast in stereotyped images which English and French Canadians have of one another' (W. E. Lambert, 1967, p. 101); he believes that the popular argument 'on economic grounds and on the attraction of the United States' carries much less weight. In this connection R. F. Salisbury's observations (1962) of bilingualism and linguistic change in New Guinea, however, invite explanations in quite different terms. In the culturally homogeneous locality that he studies it would appear that translation (of formal speeches in the native language into a neighbouring language, of a foreign visitor's quite adequate speech into a nearly synonymous version of the *same* language, of the native language—known to the visitor—into pidgin before a reply is expected, etc.) is considered to be a form of one-upmanship. It is not necessarily reciprocated by speakers of the other neighbouring languages—who presumably for that reason are looked down upon, rather than (as one might expect elsewhere) the reverse. Translation ('a linguistic means of emphasizing the importance and public nature of the discourse') is accompanied by a good deal of bi- and tri-lingual conversation, with interpretation thrown in 'more than necessary to ensure communication'. One might choose to regard all this as a form of rationalization of deeper and more unconscious motives, especially since those who do the translating in this case speak a diminishing language. Yet at the same time many Englishmen will know the experience of trying to improve their foreign languages without being given much encouragement to do so in the countries concerned! But here we surely have another kind of rationalization . . . and indeed they abound.

Non-reciprocality in language learning and code-switching may be the rule, but more surprising perhaps are those cases of non-reciprocal intelligibility. H. Wolff's (1959) study of this phenomenon among Nigerian languages and dialects is of considerable interest. Faced with the problem of devising standardized orthographies for structurally related forms of speech, Wolff made the fairly natural starting assumption that intelligibility would be largely predictable from contrastive structural analysis. This proved in very many cases not to be so; indications of non-reciprocal intelligibility pointed rather to the disturbing play of local economic and power structures, along with feelings of 'ethnic self-sufficiency' (p. 443), giving rise to what amounted to 'pecking orders of intelligibility'. As Wolff points out, the nature of intelligibility itself is all too little understood.

Code-switching can be difficult even when each code is well known. The problem is often that of *when* to switch in circumstances where cultural meanings or values seem to clash. N. Tanner (1967) discusses the example of 'low' and 'high' Javanese according to the scales of power and solidarity. If, however, she goes on to ask, two speakers are both young adults of the same age, good friends, neighbours, both with similar educational backgrounds, and sincere Moslems (all of which call for 'low' Javanese), yet of opposite sexes, married, and of different class backgrounds (calling for 'high' Javanese), which variety is to be chosen? The standard language is Indonesian; the response 'when in doubt, use Indonesian' is therefore understandable; Indonesian presents itself here as a 'neutral' language that in its everyday aspect need convey neither respect, disrespect, familiarity, nor unfamiliarity—altogether well suited to fall back upon. It is for the same reason well suited to initiate conversation —one slips in a few words of another (perhaps more intimate) code, so as to test for reactions. This is a real strength in a standard language, gained very often through its not being the vernacular of any one prominent ethnic group.

Javanese styles themselves are highly stratified, and demand considerable skill in code-switching. There would seem to be three basic levels, interlocked with each other by a special group of honorific words capable of raising the lower levels to a higher (C. Geertz, 1960, p. 248 ff.). Communication across the various 'class dialects' so formed very often demands non-reciprocal use of two of the three levels, with appropriate honorifics, choice of which—as we have seen—may or may not be entirely self-evident to their users. As Geertz puts it, 'A complete list of the determinants of level selection would . . . involve a thorough analysis of the whole framework of Javanese culture' (p. 258).

Code-switching among or within languages demands therefore constant judgment on the part of the language user, judgment which can easily go astray. J. Berry (1962, p. 221) describes the various types of English in use in Sierra Leone: standard, regional (Sierra Leone or West African?), Krio (an English-based creole), West African pidgin English, and marginal languages spoken between expatriates and their servants. Europeans here do not always properly identify the variety they learn to use, and hence convey meanings not intended, particularly, for example, when creoles are confused with pidgins (on pidgins and creoles, see p. 91).

The meaning that inheres in intra-language code-switching is well reflected in the very interesting and meticulous work of W. Labov. Labov's main concern has been with urban dialects in New York City, having regard to observable variation in the phonetic shape of five phonological 'variables': (r), (eh), (oh), (th)—i.e. voiceless, and (dh)—i.e. voiced: final or preconsonantal (r) may be realized by zero or by /r/; (eh) by /ɪə/ all the way to /aː/, (th) by /t/ through to /θ/, and (dh) correspondingly by /d/ to /ð/. It is important to note that Labov makes full use of results from an earlier sociological survey of the city—conducted by sociologists—as a base from which to make a *linguistic* study of how people speak. Sociological expertise is essential, for example, in overcoming the difficulty of apportioning individuals to more than one group in society—yet somehow reconciling such groupings. Socio-economic classification is only one possibility, itself fragmenting into several characteristics, each acquired, moreover, at different times in a person's life: educational level, occupation, income, etc.; cases of 'status incongruence' are not at all infrequent; and these are of course likely to be reflected in linguistic behaviour.

3

Labov shows, too, that social mobility is a strong candidate to put alongside measurements of the social status quo. Much of one's language behaviour, that is to say, is probably normative, in the sense of conforming to one's own ideas of the norms of the group one *aspires* to rather than the performance of the group one *belongs* to. From an anthropological angle, W. H. Goodenough (1961) makes the same point in stressing the 'intense concern' of individuals with the various symbols (which are more than 'mere markers') by which they might prove to themselves and to the world at large that they are achieving appropriate goals of 'social identity'. In a sense, a very important key to the schoolchild's language performance is precisely his notions (however ill-founded) of where, socially, he is (or would like to be) heading. Labov notes a much closer correspondence between 'lower middle class upward mobility type' and 'upper middle class' speech (at any rate in respect of the particular variants studied) than between the former and 'lower middle class stable mobility type', the former also showing the strongest subjective endorsement of the norms concerned (1966b). Indeed—and this is a fact that need surprise no one in principle (what is missing are descriptive and explanatory studies)—choice among variants of this sort reveals a great deal about a person's self-awareness, his awareness of his audience and of third parties (on the effect of an audience, see esp. A. D. Grimshaw, 1966), the heightening of such awareness in formal interview situations and its lapse—even in an interview situation—when the topic of conversation is allowed to become very personal (a factor which Labov illustrates quite graphically in 1965, p. 96 ff.), the physical 'cues' which tell the observer just how relaxed the speaker is (1964), and so forth. Perhaps Labov's most suggestive finding is that evaluative norms among New Yorkers are very much more uniform, particularly among the 18–39 age group, than their actual performance (1965, p. 84 ff.; 1966a, p. 190); moreover, the speaker tends to hear himself as using the norm that he considers correct. But possibly of equal significance are certain 'contrary directions' characteristic of 'a sizeable group of Negro speakers, Puerto Ricans, and lower class white speakers who live in close contact with these other groups' (1965, p. 96).

Labov's work shows not only the socially diagnostic importance of structurally very minor variants but also the, at least, occasional irrelevance of the concept of a language as an integrated and discrete system. In many cases it becomes difficult to talk of 'code-switching'; at any rate 'codes' will seem to ramify under inspection. J. J. Gumperz (1958) noted 'code-switching styles' of Hindi and Punjabi spoken in Delhi appropriate to specific social roles in which contact is made with the other language. A great deal of grammatical and lexical interference is tolerated, while no differences at all in phonemic inventory appear to be observable (this is not the case when the two languages are used separately). Gumperz suggests that the situation differs little from what occurs in the development of pidgins. Code-switching styles of these languages are low in prestige, and un-certain (for their users) in identity. As in the case of the 'low' style in diglossia, they do not attract scholarly descriptive analysis, except by the outsider. Gumperz himself finds interesting possibilities for more economical and exact description in terms of shared rules and (lower-level) non-shared rules. When bi-linguals interact with other bilinguals new norms of correctness are generated (1967a, 1967b). Gumperz may well be making a significant point when he remarks that differences between languages in contact may very often be of such a kind as to be more noticeable for their users (allowing them to stress their distinctness as languages) than in fact an actual hindrance to communication (1967a, p. 56). At the same time, there is as we have seen the possibly more important converse case in which differences (including those within the one language) which tend *not* to be noticeable do hinder communication in certain important respects—and possibly for this very reason.

The linguistic convergence of languages in frequent contact takes the form of code-switching and/or integration and/or inter-ference; the last as well as the first of these is well exemplified by Gumperz (1958), even though he rejects from such situations what he regards as a criterial attribute of interference, namely the direct and imperfect imitation of an unmixed standard form of a language. But it is difficult to see why one should look at interference like this. From the standpoint of the individual language user, the process is bound to become one in which false imitation perpetuates itself. Pidgins are an extreme case, and develop through rapid reciprocal imitation.

W. H. Whiteley's revealing study of the structure and status of English loanwords among Swahili speakers in Dar-es-Salaam (W. H. Whiteley, 1967) shows a picture of coexistent systems or patterns of assimilation at phonological and morphological levels according to the education (including knowledge of English) and outlook of the speaker, the subject of discourse, and the nature of the social context. One would like to know more about a type of language flexibility of which the author gives a hint, namely the very free shifting which may be observed among bilinguals between unassimilated and assimilated loans, as for example from 'Regional Commissioner' in one sentence to 'Rejenokamíshna' in the next (p. 129). One suspects the interplay (including perhaps deliberate counterbalancing) of cultural values just as much as in code-switching over longer stretches; just as much, too, as in English when we shift, meaningfully, from one form of personal address or reference to another, or interject the word 'sir' *occasionally*; always accepting, however, the fact that borrowing of any sort is not a straightforward importation of aspects of the other culture. As T. E. Hope (1962–3, p. 39) has observed, a receiving language exploits a semiological pattern already established in another idiom, realized in terms of its own collocations, but in exploiting these during an all-important interim period develops its *own* contexts and hence changes in meaning. New efficiency in handling old concepts also takes its place beside the importation of new concepts, and both may be largely independent of acculturation. It has already been pointed out that bilingualism (or language learning) and biculturalism need not occur together; the same principle holds good in the case of borrowing.

Directions of borrowing among bilinguals can be interesting. Sango, a creolized lingua franca which serves a large number of people in the Central African Republic for the oral and written dissemination of communications of all kinds, borrows words, according to W. J. Samarin (1966), from vernaculars, yet vernacular speakers themselves will tend not to accept as Sango words borrowed from their *own* vernacular. For those ignorant of French, the élite official language, Sango represents the only escape from vernaculars that seem to their users to connote rural inferiority. Samarin regards Sango as a very conformist language that effectively conceals its speakers' origins. Code-switching between the vernaculars and Sango again illustrates therefore how choice of language is often so much bound up with choice of social identity and with social values.

'Social group', with particular reference to linguistic correlates, is approached from various angles in:

BERNSTEIN, B. (1960). 'Language and social class', in *British Journal of Sociology*.

BERNSTEIN, B. (1961a). 'Social class and linguistic development: a theory of social learning', in *Society, Economy and Education*, eds. Floud, J., Halsey, A. H. and Anderson, A.

BERNSTEIN, B. (1961b). 'Social structure, language and learning', in *Educational Research*, 3, 3.

BERNSTEIN, B. (1961c). 'Aspects of language of the social process', in Hymes, D. H. (1964c).

BERNSTEIN, B. (1962). 'Linguistic codes, hesitation phenomena and intelligence', in *Language and Speech*, 5, 1.

BERNSTEIN, B. (1964). 'Social class, speech systems and psychotherapy', in *British Journal of Sociology*.

BERNSTEIN, B. (1966). 'Elaborated and restricted codes', in *Sociological Inquiry*, Spring number entitled *Explorations in Socio-Linguistics*.

BROOK, G. L. (1964). *English Dialects*, ch. 7.

FERGUSON, C. A. (1959). 'Diglossia', in Hymes, D. H. (1964c).

GUMPERZ, J. J. (1958). 'Hindi-Punjabi code-switching in Delhi', in *Proceedings of the VIII International Congress of Linguists*.

GUMPERZ, J. J. (1961). 'Speech variation and the study of Indian civilization', in Hymes, D. H. (1964c).

GUMPERZ, J. J. (1962). 'Language problems in the rural development of North India', in *Study of the Role of Second Languages*, ed. Rice, F. A.

GUMPERZ, J. J. (1964). 'Linguistic and social interaction in two communities', in *American Anthropologist*, 66, 6, 2.

HAAS, M. R. (1944). 'Men's and women's speech in Koasati', in Hymes, D. H. (1964c).

HALLIDAY, M. A. K., McINTOSH, A. and STREVENS, P. D. (1964). *The Linguistic Sciences and Language Teaching*, ch. 4.

HAUGEN, E. (1956). *Bilingualism in the Americas*.

HAUGEN, E. (1962). 'Schizoglossia and the linguistic norm', in *Monograph Series on Languages and Linguistics*.

KENYON, J. S. (1948). 'Cultural levels and functional varieties of English', in Allen, H. B., *Readings in Applied English Linguistics*.

KLEIN, J. (1965). *Samples from English Culture*.

LABOV, W. (1963). 'The social motivation of a sound change', in *Word*.

LABOV, W. (1964). 'Phonological correlates of social stratification', in *American Anthropologist*, 66, 2.

LABOV, W. (1965). 'Stages in the acquisition of standard English', in Shuy, R. W. (1965), *Social Dialects and Language Learning*.

LABOV, W. (1966a). 'The effect of social mobility on linguistic behaviour', in *Sociological Inquiry*, Spring.

LABOV, W. (1966b). *The Social Stratification of English in New York City*.

MARCKWARDT, A. H. and QUIRK, R. (1964). *A Common Language*.

NEWMAN, S. (1964). 'Vocabulary levels: Zuni sacred and slang usage', in Hymes, D. H. (1964c).

PICKFORD, G. R. (1956). 'American linguistic geography', in *Word*.

PUTNAM, G. N. and O'HERN, E. M. (1955). *The Status Significance of an Isolated Urban Dialect:* Supplement of *Language*, vol. 31.

SAMARIN, W. J. (1966). 'Self-annulling prestige factors among speakers of a Creole language', in Bright, W. (1966).

SAPIR, E. (1921). *Language*.

SAPIR, E. (1931b). 'Dialect', in Mandelbaum, D. G., ed. *Selected Writings of Edward Sapir*.

SAPIR, E. (1933). 'Language', in Mandelbaum, D. G. (as above).

SCHATZMAN, L. and STRAUSS, A. (1955). 'Social class and modes of communication', in *American Journal of Sociology*.

SHUY, R. W., ed. (1965). *Social Dialects and Language Learning*.

SPROTT, W. J. H. (1958). *Human Groups*.

STEWART, W. A., ed. (1964). *Non-standard Speech and the Teaching of English*.

STEWART, W. A. (1965). 'Urban Negro speech: sociolinguistic factors affecting English teaching', in Shuy, R. W. (1965).

# 5 Standard and Vernacular Language Functions

The problem of specifying the general nature of linguistically signalled social values takes on further significance when it comes to the study of the selection, codification, acceptance, and functional elaboration of standard languages (see E. Haugen, 1966a and 1966c). Standard languages can arise from three main sources: first, from the promotion of a language largely used outside the speech community to the role of a superimposed medium of communication, in cases where none of the several indigenous languages or dialects is considered suitable; second from the selection of one particular local dialect from two or more candidates; and third, from the standardization of some form of 'mixed' language.

It has not infrequently been pointed out that three basic factors have to be weighed together by the community concerned, namely the need to reinforce the *unification* of the community itself, to assert its *separation* from outside neighbours, and to ensure its ability to communicate *internationally* (see for example P. L. Garvin, 1959; and E. Haugen, 1966a). The first two of these are clearly aspects of group solidarity, the last an aspect of the need for prestige and power—the power that is naturally conferred by any 'window on the world'. What strikes one about each particular locale, however, is again the particularity or even uniqueness of what these very general considerations entail.

E. Haugen (1959, 1966c) provides a thought-provoking account of the then standard language situation in Norway, where the rival varieties of 'bokmål' and 'nynorsk' can be spoken of, without too much risk of over-simplification, as 'more civilized' and 'more Norwegian' respectively. Such factors as prestige, power, solidarity, etc., will no doubt, in the course of time, contribute to the emergence of the one or the other, or some fusion of the two, as standard, but meanwhile it is worth pondering the fact that government support (reflected, for example, in educational policy) has not effectively checked the decline of 'nynorsk' since 1945. Even so, if Haugen is right in pointing to the 'urban sub-standard' bridge variety as the nascent standard language, then one may still be witnessing the long-term but conceivably inevitable success of relatively low-prestige everyday communicative efficiency (and of course commercial utility) over a relatively high-prestige form of language. The survival of English rather than French after 1066 also helps to undermine the generalization that the more prestigeful language will always displace the less prestigeful (see J. A. Fishman, 1966, pp. 444, 445, for several other examples); and so too (closer to the Norwegian case) does the story of the origins of modern Standard English in south-eastern dialects of apparently low social status yet high utility value

The development of a standard language is particularly difficult to predict or control in a situation of 'diglossia'. This term was used by C. A. Ferguson (1959) to apply to a situation in which two varieties of a single language fulfil distinctly complementary and stable roles within the same speech community—the one with higher prestige ('the vehicle of a large and respected body of written literature') learned largely through formal education, and generally used for formal purposes, the other the normal medium of everyday conversation. These are often referred to as 'high' (H) and 'low' (L) forms of the language respectively. Diglossia is and always has been an extremely widespread phenomenon, particularly if its definition is widened to allow for the complementary functioning of two *languages* within the same speech community.

It can readily be appreciated that stability under such circumstances is not necessarily or wholly a desirable state of affairs. Over-regard for aesthetic, logical, and other qualities thought to inhere in H, feelings of protectiveness towards it which inhibit borrowing, non-use in relaxed casual encounters, above all the fact that it has to be taught rather like a second language at school, are functional disadvantages perhaps greater even than those of L—which are namely its tendency to dialectal dispersion, low prestige, and inadequacy for higher academic purposes. All these disadvantages are particularly severe when demands for literacy and a unifying language are in the air. Diglossia therefore presents an interesting aspect of the far-reaching question of whether or not a 'functional relativity' holds among languages. D. H. Hymes (1961b) expresses the view that evolutionary equality among existing languages is evident only in the sense of *potential* equality. He wishes to distinguish between non-existent 'primitive' languages, 'full' languages, and 'advanced' languages. In this light diglossia would seem to be one possible (but not necessary) characteristic for a full, but not of an advanced language. But one must bear in mind, too, those cases where either H or L (normally H) is used outside the given speech community (for example, Standard German outside Switzerland, French outside Haiti, etc.). Potentialities for its functional development within the community will clearly be all the greater in such circumstances.

This will *only* be potentially so, however. In December 1964 the writer had occasion to make a rather rapid assessment of the classroom linguistic experience of Somali school pupils, in order to make recommendations which might bear upon a re-assessment of the educational linguistic policy of the country, with special reference to the creation of a national university ('Somalia', 1965). The Somali Republic is admittedly more nearly homogeneous, linguistically speaking, than most other African states, but from the point of view of individual bilingualism it would appear to present an extremely heterogeneous picture. The mother-tongues are Somali, Rahanwiin (unintelligible to Somali speakers: B. W. Andrzejewski, 1962; J. J. Pia, 1966), and a Bantu language, Chimini. In terms of numbers speaking each mother-tongue language, one might agree with Andrzejewski and Pia in regarding Somalia as a basically monolingual country, that is mainly speaking Somali. However, three outside languages (Arabic, Italian, and English) are used for certain purposes and by certain groups and are used as media of instruction in certain parts of the educational system—each one in *some* degree, particularly Arabic, qualifying as a 'high' form of language. Arabic presents on top of this, however, its own picture of diglossia, in that the young Somali has somehow to learn both Classical *and* Colloquial Arabic. It is not uncommon for a Somali to handle—for various purposes, but very largely also as a consequence of his schooling—each or any of Arabic, English, Italian, and at least his own dialect of the vernacular Somali. Some also speak Swahili, the primary 'vehicular' language of East Africa. Each returning graduate or school-leaver from overseas, moreover, is liable to speak at least one other language. The socio-linguistic facts are likely therefore to be complex.

It is clear that linguistic planning for the educational system could alter the whole picture quite radically (see Appendix to Chapter 11). Yet at the same time, as E. Haugen (1966c) has stressed, it is what the bulk of the population wants that matters most in the long run. From this point of view the readily observable fact that Italian is still very widely used indeed for everyday commercial purposes in Somalia may well be less important for the future than the economically and numerically much less impressive tendency among the adult population at large to enrol for adult literacy classes in English—which in terms of observable use comes off rather badly in comparison not only with Italian, but with Somali and Arabic as well. The visitor to Somalia is likely to be strikingly impressed by the effectiveness of the English usage of very young school pupils in the countryside in the south, where English is not employed as the medium of instruction at this level.

A functionally powerful language, as English is in so many of its far-flung territories, will readily and usefully accept diversification into many kinds of variety or style. Indonesian for example is undergoing rapid functional elaboration. This of course is a very much more complex process than any mere absorption of highly technical terms, and even at the lexical level one can appreciate the difficulty of incorporating the full meanings of those many scientific words that are not restricted to a particular science; such words as: assume, constant, intensity, method, series, vary, compensate, correspond, correlate, element, extinction, field, normal, range, ratio, relative, structure, theory, variation, etc. (see further C. L. Barber, 1962). More important is the need for functional diversity in the standardization of a language. Indonesian is expanding not least in what Weinreich called a 'slangy anti-prestige' direction as well as in response to modern technological and scientific needs. Hindi also ranges through many varieties, from a formal literary idiom through standard spoken Hindi and many 'regional standards' to forms of village Hindi which themselves often possess both a conversational and an oratorical style incorporating Sanskrit loan words (see J. J. Gumperz, 1962, for example).

The possibility of *deliberate* mixing of languages, dialects or varieties to produce a standard language sometimes arises. But there are curious aspects to this solution. F. W. Householder (1962) observes of Greek diglossia that 'Discussion of vocabulary is a very important part of Greek folk culture as a whole, and grammar plays almost no part, relatively speaking' (p. 131). Yet the real structural and social dichotomy itself is not lexical so much as grammatical (as in most or all cases of diglossia: see for example C. A. Ferguson, 1959; W. A. Stewart, 1962b). It would seem as if an inverse relationship holds between *awareness* of structural likeness and unlikeness and its symbolic *importance*; any such relationship would of course be an illustration of the notion that language, because and when it belongs with other largely subconscious activities, is in Boas's words 'almost potent in the formation of our opinions and actions' (F. Boas, 1911, p. 20).

The still controversial 'linguistic relativity' hypothesis associated with the name of B. L. Whorf takes Boas's standpoint a stage further. In the words of J. B. Carroll and J. B. Casagrande (1958), 'The linguistic relativity hypothesis is a special case of the culture-personality theory . . . each language . . . develops special ways of communicating. These ways of communicating create special needs, special responses, and lead to the development of special modes of thinking. The alternative to the linguistic relativity hypothesis would be a statement that the behaviour of a person is not a function of the language he happens to speak or be speaking, that his modes of categorizing experience and dealing with his world operate independently of language, that language is simply a way of communicating something which is in every way prior to its codification in language' (p. 20). As D. H. Hymes (1961a) puts it: 'One will find other statements of this view, ranging from the sweepingly provocative to the gently urbane' (p. 325). Now however far one agrees or disagrees with the more extreme expressions of the notions of linguistic relativity, it seems true to say that those aspects of language of which we are least consciously aware are by no means necessarily the least important. It may be difficult therefore to plan for the merging of two systems the really important features of which are the most difficult to perceive. It is no doubt relatively easy to manipulate mere items of vocabulary, extend their contexts, coin new words and so forth; but in doing so the root of the matter may very well be left untouched. Closer home one has only to think of the far-reaching differences in the grammars of English social dialects, differences of which not everybody is fully aware, as Bernstein has repeatedly argued.

The linguistic relativity perspective emphasizes the unique value of a small and seemingly insignificant vernacular language. J. Reinecke's quotation (see D. H. Hymes, 1964c, p. 540) from an eighteenth-century description of Haiti expresses the matter well: 'There are a thousand things one dares not say in French, a thousand voluptuous images which one can hardly render successfully, which the Creole expresses or renders with infinite grace.' There is strong feeling here for something that French *could not* supply in that environment and for those people. B. W.

Andrzejewski has a series of articles on the significant role of
verbal art in Somali, which is another vernacular language
labouring under a form of diglossia, where not one but three
alien languages compete for the position of H. Not only are
oral poems and proverbs quoted on formal occasions, but in
everyday conversation great care (nurtured in the very young)
is taken to establish inter-personal relations in a suitably indirect,
subtle, and frequently allusive manner. Such everyday diplomacy
is less a part of our own society, and in any case may well be
substantially different in kind (a difference which, incidentally,
poses problems for the translation of oral literatures which are
often not faced or even recognized—with the result that African
oral arts, languages, and general mentalities can seem quite
wrongly to be barbaric and naïve: B. W. Andrzejewski 1965).

In Burundi, the 'manipulation of emotions by aesthetic devices
is the principal business of speech behaviour'; these are highly
stylized forms of speaking (which again are trained early), elaborate and aesthetically judged ways of expressing disagreement
with one's superiors, petitioning for a gift, and so forth.
These and other functions are not incidental but rather
quite central to the culture concerned (E. M. Albert, 1964).
E. E. Evans-Pritchard (1956; see also 1963, 1964) provides a
revealing if possibly biased account of 'sanza'-talk among the
Zande of the Sudan: this is the language of dissimulation, hinting,
circumlocution, innuendo, sarcasm, in general the deployment
of those (partly gestural) argument-clinching remarks which
cannot be proved by their recipient to be directly intended as
such . . . Evans-Pritchard believes that the use of the same formal
label for this as well as for oral proverbs suggests their identity
in meaning or intention, but whether this is so or not Zande
proverbs are not only unusually significant for everyday discourse but also acquire meaning against the background of
local social life, physical surroundings, and folk-tales. The
proverb has been called a short sentence drawn from long
experience. This is a good description; difficulties in interpretation by the outsider merely serve to epitomize the uniqueness

of the experience that goes into their making and the making of their languages.

References pertaining to 'standard' languages, 'vernaculars', and 'diglossia' (in alphabetical order):

BRIGHT, W. and RAMANUJAN, A. K. (1962). 'Socio-linguistic variation and language change', in *Proceedings of the IX International Congress of Linguists*. Discusses in particular the role of literacy as a prestige factor countering linguistic innovation; the case of Iceland is referred to in the ensuing discussion by E. Haugen.

BROSNAHAN, L. F. (1963). 'Some historical cases of language imposition', in Spencer, J., ed. *Language in Africa*.

BULL, W. E. (1955). 'The use of vernacular languages in fundamental education', in Hymes, D. H. (1964c). Highly critical of the assumption in UNESCO (1953) that 'the best medium for teaching is the mother tongue of the pupil'. Stresses the limitations of vernaculars, and difficulties involved in the rapid extension of their usefulness. Compare Hymes, D. H. (1961b) 'Functions of speech', in *Anthropology and Education*, ed. Gruber, F. C. A different view is taken by Hall, R. A. (1966). *Pidgin and Creole Languages*, ch. 10.

FERGUSON, C. A. (1959). 'Diglossia', in Hymes, D. H. (1964c).

FERGUSON, C. A. (1962b). 'Principles of teaching languages with diglossia', in *Monograph Series on Languages and Linguistics*.

FERGUSON, C. A. (1964a). 'On sociologically oriented language surveys', in *Linguistic Reporter*, 8, 4.

FERGUSON, C. A. (1966b). 'National socio-linguistic profile formulas', in Bright, W. (ed.) *Socio-linguistics*.

FISHMAN, J. A. (1967). 'Bilingualism with and without diglossia; diglossia with and without bilingualism', in *Journal of Social Issues*, vol. 23, no. 2.

GARVIN, P. L. (1959). 'The standard language problem', in Hymes, D. H. (1964c). Properties necessary for a standard language. Compare Haugen, E. (1966c) below.

GARVIN, P. L. and MATHIOT, M. (1960). 'The urbanization of the Guarani language', in Wallace, A. F. C., ed. *Men and Cultures*.

GUMPERZ, J. J. and NAIM, C. M. (1960). 'Formal and informal standards in the Hindi language area', in Ferguson, C. A. and Gumperz, J. J. (1960).

GUMPERZ, J. J. (1961). 'Speech variation and the study of Indian civilization', in Hymes, D. H. (1964c).

HALL, R. A. (1966). *Pidgin and Creole Languages*, 131 ff.

HAUGEN, E. (1956). *Bilingualism in the Americas*.

HAUGEN, E. (1959). 'Planning for a standard language in modern Norway', in *Anthropological Linguistics*, 1, 3.

HAUGEN, E. (1962). 'Schizoglossia and the linguistic norm', in *Monograph Series on Languages and Linguistics*. Georgetown University.

HAUGEN, E. (1966a). 'Language, dialect, nation', in *American Anthropologist*, 68, 4. Properties necessary for a standard language, all or some of which are lacking in a vernacular.

HAUGEN, E. (1966b). 'Linguistics and language planning', in Bright, W. (1966) *Socio-linguistics*. Emphasizes the role of the written language in language planning; description and creation of a norm; planning for diversity as well as for uniformity; difficulty in learning versus difficulty in use; enrichment of the standard language by the study of dialects; 'prestige', the role of the linguist.

HAUGEN, E. (1966c). *Language Conflict and Language Planning*. Harvard University Press.

HOUSEHOLDER, F. W. (1962). 'Greek diglossia', in *Monograph Series on Languages and Linguistics*.

HYMES, D. H. (1961b). 'Functions of speech: an evolutionary approach', in *Anthropology and Education*, ed. Gruber, F. C.

HYMES, D. H. (1964c). *Language in Culture and Society*. See esp. the large 'topical bibliography' on pp. 523–6.

LE PAGE, R. B. (1964). *The National Language Question*, 21 ff. On the use of vernacular languages in education; pros and cons for the use of the vernacular, short-term and long-term.

MOULTON, W. G. (1962). 'What standard for diglossia? The case of German Switzerland', in *Monograph Series on Language and Linguistics*.

PERREN, G. E. and HOLLOWAY, M. F. (1965). *Language and Communication in the Commonwealth*.

RAY, P. S. (1963). *Language Standardisation*.

STERN, H. H. (1962). *Foreign Languages in Primary Education*.

STEWART, W. A. (1962a). 'An outline of linguistic typology for describing multilingualism', in *Study of the Role of Second Languages*, ed. Rice.

STEWART, W. A. (1962c). 'The functional distribution of Creole and French in Haiti', in *Monograph Series on Languages and Linguistics*.

TRIM, J. L. M. (1961). 'English standard pronunciation', in *English Language Teaching*, 16, 1.

WEINREICH, U. (1953). *Languages in Contact*.

WOLFF, H. (1959). 'Intelligibility and inter-ethnic attitudes', in Hymes, D. H. (1964c).

On inter-language 'linguistic relativity':

BOAS, F. (1911). 'Linguistics and ethnology', in Hymes, D. H. (1964c), 17 ff.

DIEBOLD, A. R. (1964). Review of Sol Saporta, *Psycholinguistics*, in *Language*.

HYMES, D. H. (1961a). 'Linguistic aspects of cross-cultural personality study', in *Studying Personality Cross-Culturally*, ed. Kaplan, B., 324–37.

HYMES, D. H. (1961b). 'Functions of speech', in *Anthropology and Education*, ed. Gruber, F. C., 59, 60.

HYMES, D. H. (1964c). *Language in Culture and Society*, Part III. See also p. 5–11, where the distinction is drawn between languages as 'a socially inherited system . . . seen primarily in terms of the cognitive function of distinguishing or expressing meanings', and as activity in social contexts.

LENNEBERG, E. H. (1953). 'Cognition in ethnolinguistics', in *Language*.

LENNEBERG, E. H. (1962). 'The relationship of language to formation of concepts', in *Synthese*, 14.

LYONS, J. (1963a). *Structural Semantics*, 39, 40, 80–7.

SAPIR, E. (1924). 'The grammarian and his language', in *Selected Writings of Edward Sapir*, ed. Mandelbaum, D. G.

SAPIR, E. (1933). 'Language', in D. G. Mandelbaum.

SPENCE, N. C. W. (1964). 'The basic problems in ethnolinguistics', in *Archivum Linguisticum*.

WHORF, B. L. See *Language, Thought and Reality*, ed. Carroll, J. B.

On intra-language 'linguistic relativity':

BELLUGI, U. and BROWN, R. (1964). *The Acquisition of Language (Monographs of The Society for Research in Child Development)*, 109, 110.

BERNSTEIN, B. (1965). 'A socio-linguistic approach to social learning', in *Penguin Survey of the Social Sciences 1965*.

HYMES, D. H. (1961a). See above, 341 ff.

HYMES, D. H. (1964a). 'Towards ethnographies of communication', in *American Anthropologist*, 19 ff.

HYMES, D. H. (1964d). Comments on a paper by M. Bullowa, in Bellugi, U. and Brown, R. *The Acquisition of Language.*

KLEIN, J. (1965). *Samples from English Culture.*

LAWTON, D. (1963). 'Social class differences in language development', in *Language and Speech*, 6, 3.

LAWTON, D. (1964). 'Social class language difference in group discussions', in *Language and Speech*, 7, 3.

ROBINSON, W. P. (1965a). 'Cloze procedure as a technique for the investigation of social class differences in language usage', in *Language and Speech*, 8, 1.

ROBINSON, W. P. (1965b). 'The elaborated code in working class language', in *Language and Speech*, 8, 2.

SCHATZMAN, L. and STRAUSS, A. (1955). 'Social class and modes of communication', in *American Journal of Sociology.*

ULLMANN, S. (1962). *Semantics*, 243 ff., esp. p. 252.

# 6 Speech Functions

Suppose one were to make a comparative study of different styles of a given language. What features should one compare?— All the grammar, or some of the grammar, the lexis, or what? One could go about it this way, certainly, but there is also good reason to choose as one's point or points of comparison something like what Firth called 'speech functions': 'commands', 'requests', 'invitations', 'suggestions', 'advice', 'offers of assistance', 'gratitude', 'agreement and disagreement', 'greeting', 'leave-taking', 'encouragement', 'permission', 'promising', 'apology', 'threats', 'warning', 'insulting', 'pleading', and so forth. There are very many such terms in the everyday language (one might compare, on a different plane, G. W. Allport's collection of 18,000 terms in English referring to personality characteristics). Most can be switched from 'giving' to 'asking for' (advice, etc.); made negative or positive; conveyed or recognized by a mere word, or a tone perhaps, or alternatively be only apparent at the end of the chapter or six months later or between the lines, or through all of these means together; understood or not understood in the manner intended; deliberately ambiguous or otherwise: and so forth.

Purposes of this general sort can be variously social or individual in character, and are not easy to categorize. 'Power', 'solidarity', and other such relationships attend one more or less continuously, and it is by comparison very intermittently indeed that we give orders, strike up or discourage acquantanceships, say goodbye, express agreement, and so on. These last are recurrent but non-continuous functions: a man may be a manager of a firm and talk about certain things only, exercise power, etc., for six hours, but no more, every day—and then switch to other domains, topics, and relationships. Firth himself chose to refer to the more intermittent activities as 'speech functions', reserving for such categories as 'familiar, colloquial, and more formal speech', or 'the language of the School, the Law, the Church, and all the specialized forms of speech', the term 'speech situations'. He does not, however, use the two expressions very clearly, since as examples of the latter he includes 'such common situations' as 'address', 'greetings, farewells or mutual recognition of status or relationship on contact, adjustment of relations after contact, breaking off relations, renewal of relations, change of relations', etc.—all of which may equally well be regarded as speech functions.

The selection of speech functions as points of reference for comparison is not a popular strategy. Labov's approach would seem to strike most linguists as more linguistic; he seeks to show how, for example, as we have seen, the first consonant of 'thing', 'thought', etc., is realized as stop, affricate, or fricative. One might question, however, whether these variables are as interesting, either linguistically or sociologically, as the varied linguistic realization of such everyday purposes as those we have been referring to; such realization will tend to be very much less atomistic and homogeneous, yet still admit of linguistic description. *Sociologically* speaking, the adoption of more functional points of reference might, one suspects, throw if not more light at least a different light on the structure of society which one thereby infers. Indeed, it seems fairly apparent that misinterpretation of the various intended meanings of say an innocent request like 'You couldn't change half-a-crown for me, could you?' can often be far less noticeable to either participant yet far more disturbing than the temporary unintelligibility or gross social judgments that attend the use of /t/ instead of /θ/, etc.

There seems little doubt about the likelihood of 'interference' among different social groups in the native language in these respects. The sociologist T. Burns found that in a group of eight firms in Edinburgh there were wide discrepancies between management and staff in their understanding of whether messages were intended on the one hand to be 'instructions and decisions' or on the other 'information and advice' (T. Burns, 1957). Total misunderstanding occurred, or seemed to occur, on almost half the relevant occasions. But there the matter rests, without linguistic investigation into why this should have been so. Intuition tells us that we all trip up some of the time in precisely such respects, especially across social barriers; and of course this is a really persistent type of problem facing the overseas learner of any language. There may be many such problems well known to all sorts of people which have nevertheless not been translated into more technically linguistic terms. G. Vickers (1955, p. 78) states that many communications in industry have no other object or effect than to 'create confidence', and that these play a much larger part within 'working societies' (including trade unions and the like) than elsewhere. About the early stages of the National Coal Board, Vickers writes: 'When opinions, orders and information began to fly up and down these newly improvised channels, everyone concerned found at first a curious difficulty in making himself understood.'

It is important to note that the expression of speech functions, even in an interview situation, is likely to be not less but more immune from those stereotyped patterns of 'conscious suppression' or censorship (amounting to 'hyper-correction') that Labov is anxious to avoid or control. At the same time, much of their interest derives from the ways in which choice tends to be, as often as not, semi-conscious and semi-deliberate. Leave-taking repertoires, for example, are not arrived at or handled quickly or easily. Who among us has not caught himself at some time or another trying to get away, casting around in his mind for the right formula, the odd word or two, or long story for that matter, that does the trick smoothly and acceptably? J. R. Firth (1935) undoubtedly had this sort of thing in mind when he wrote that 'conversation is much more of a roughly prescribed ritual than most people think'. The term 'ritual' here should not mislead one into thinking of such choices as straightforward. Slotting into the *right* ritual in such respects is not entirely easy, nor entirely conscious, and in many ways can be extremely revealing.

The relatively slight attention that has so far been paid to these matters has tended to be rather discursive or programmatic. R. Jakobson's spectrum of functions according to relative focus on the various constituents of the speech event (R. Jakobson, 1960) has the merit of showing that linguistics might have something to say in this area, even if it means that discrete yes/no alternatives are less in evidence than the continuous gradience which also characterizes the expression of emotive elements and the like. Jakobson's scheme has been taken up more recently by D. Hymes (1964a, p. 21 ff.), who wishes description of the speech event to entail a very comprehensive set of factors indeed. In Hymes's paper the general stress laid on 'inner structural relations and purpose' (p. 22) does not carry with it, however, any particular emphasis on what we are calling speech functions. B. Malinowski (1935) clearly articulated the view that 'pragmatic' functions stand very near the heart of language in use; indeed 'it is the pragmatic use of speech within the context of action which has shaped its structure' (p. 52). Whether or not one has regard for Malinowski's structural descriptions (see J. R. Firth, 1957), the question should still be asked whether the structure of each language might not answer quite fundamentally to functions of this sort, the expression of which, after all, is developed from the very earliest stages of language acquisition.

The term 'pragmatics' itself, which is particularly associated with Malinowski's view of language, flits in and out of this general area of concern. As U. Weinreich (1963) points out, the field of pragmatics has 'virtually no conventional content' (p. 150 and fn. 12). D. H. Hymes (1964a, p. 10) relates the possibility of a 'structural pragmemics' to the total set of functions which he derives from Jakobson. J. H. Greenberg had earlier (1948) drawn much the same picture as that of Hymes for the pragmatic dimension of language, placing it alongside the 'syntactic' and the 'semantic', but in the realm of 'parole' rather than of 'langue'.

In this context, U. Weinreich's handling of what is pragmatic in language appears to be relevant to a consideration of speech

functions, although perhaps somewhat unnecessarily involved
(U. Weinreich, 1963). First of all, he wishes to restrict its coverage
to that 'paradigm of discourse features which comprise assertion,
and features incompatible with assertion and with each other:
question, command, and attitudes to the content of discourse,
in so far as they are coded' (p. 150). The requirement of mutual
incompatibility would appear, however, to rule out, on one
occasion or another, even the exemplified categories—as they
appear already to have ruled out for Weinreich such functions as
'suggestion', 'advice', etc. Thus the question 'What are you
going to do about it then?' as often as not conveys what would
appear to be a clear question and a clear command simul-
taneously. Moreover, the linguistic constituents of this utterance
which express question and command so overlay one another
that 'incompatibility' would be very difficult to explain or
demonstrate. Nor do 'attitudes' easily lend themselves to an
either-this-or-that approach: approval and disapproval (p. 152)
can undoubtedly both be expressed at once, in relation to an
identical target, even in, say, particular renderings of the word
'yes'. We all sooner or later learn to express agreement simul-
taneously with disagreement, fear with longing, etc. (again see
Weinreich, p. 152), in such a way as to throw doubt on their
incompatibility—non-linguistic and linguistic alike. Weinreich's
attention seems to be resting on those highly coded and highly
codeable formal markers (verbal morphology, question particles,
etc.) that seem *on later inspection* to correspond most directly with
particular functions, rather than on 'mixed bags' of formal
features that come together in answer to functional needs.

For Weinreich then—and his is a view which marks perhaps
the nearest approach of *linguistics* to the problem of speech
functions since Firth—pragmatics is part of semantics to the
extent that its features are codeable, codeability implying the
presence of formal markers *already* described in the grammar.
A basic distinction is made between signs as 'designators' and
as 'formators', the former consisting of a sign-vehicle and a
designatum, the latter of a sign-vehicle and 'an implicit instruc-

tion for an operation, such as negation, generalization, and the like' (p. 145). 'A designatum may be said to constitute a set of conditions; in a situation in which such conditions are actually fulfilled . . . the token of the sign may be said to denote' (p. 145; compare C. Osgood's distinction in the same volume between 'denotation' and 'connotation', the latter concerning 'affective reactions to signs'). Weinreich goes on later: 'for our purposes we can apply Carnap's working definition of "designator": "all those expressions to which a semantical analysis of meaning is applied" ' (p. 149); thus 'bread' on the one hand is contrasted with 'or' and 'this' on the other as examples of designators and formators respectively—corresponding roughly therefore with a traditional notion of language as consisting of 'full' words and 'empty' words. The distinction is exemplified respectively by the cases of Thai 'hat', 'bat', meaning 'royal hand', 'royal foot', regardless of who is speaking to whom, and Tibetan 'u' and 'go', both meaning 'head', but each chosen in accordance with the attitude of the speaker to the listener or subject of discourse. The Thai words are referred to as examples of designators, the Tibetan as the formators (p. 155). Pragmatics is said to belong to the realm of formators. Formators operate upon designators, and are regarded as part of semantics, yet even so '. . . there must be a clear-cut realization that the province of linguistic semantics is the study . . . of the designational system proper to each language' (p. 191). In its rather different way this is a view of the place of linguistics which accords well with that of Katz and Fodor (1963, p. 489). It allows pragmatics, in this sense, a very marginal place in linguistics indeed.

Labels such as 'command', 'request', etc., are of course by no means easy to define. What might be a 'command' for the speaker or writer might—as we have seen—have the force of a 'request' or mere piece of 'advice' for the listener or reader. Moreover, for any one person what a 'command' is will depend on what a 'request' is, and a 'suggestion', etc. Quite intuitively speaking, however, there would still appear to be sets of terms here amounting to semantic fields in their own right, each term linked perhaps by a common denominator—one of which might informally be referred to, for example, as the intention of inducing someone else to do what one wishes him to do. Behaviouristic definition is of course quite inadequate, as we shall see in Chapter 12 in referring to Chomsky's criticism of Skinner: the two main issues being first that what the receiver does in response is not the whole point, if one thinks (as one must) of the traditional and everyday regard for the intention of the speaker (N. Chomsky, 1959, p. 567), and second that experimental methodology found useful for studying animals may be quite irrelevant when it comes to the study of human verbal behaviour. Further than this, it should not be assumed that the only kind of overt marker is the formally linguistic. There are all manner of overt 'para-linguistic' and non-linguistic markers to consider, and here as always one can only be guided in the last resort by intuitive feeling for what is meaningful, and what is not meaningful.

# 7 The Speech Event

The 'speech community' as a composite of linguistic and non-linguistic elements is matched in this respect at the level of the face-to-face encounter or 'speech event'. In discussing some of the motivations for and processes involved in choice of language (dialect, variety, style, etc.) among the members of a speech community at large one naturally does not exclude the individual as individual. What motivates him, and the way he handles language, may be idiosyncratic up to a point, yet at the same time will also reflect on a smaller scale the same larger forces; at any rate it would be difficult to show that the crucial factors entering into the verbal behaviour of the speech community do as a whole not also operate within very small groups.

The boundaries and structure of the speech event itself are complex indeed. There always seem to be little events inside big events, extended 'strands of something or other which permeate long stretches of text and produce a gradual build-up of effect' (A. McIntosh, 1965, p. 19), unnoticed transitions from one topic to the next, and so forth. All of these things, moreover, are in no small measure related to the viewpoint or focus of each of the participants themselves. This is so in a cultural sense (witness A. I. Hallowell's story of the old man diligently attending to what the Thunder Birds had to say: see D. H. Hymes, 1964a, p. 14, 15), in a generational sense (the speech events of very small children are not our own speech events), and in an everyday sense (the speech event seen as a set of 'ventures in joint orientation', a process of very imperfect sharing, each participant both creatively and conventionally structuring and restructuring his own view of things). The speech event is far removed, that is to say, from the text as merely recorded.

K. L. Pike (1954, 1967) attends to three types of participant focus: 'depth of focus' (size of the unit of behaviour perceived), 'breadth of focus' (how many units at a time), and 'height of focus' (over what stretch of time). The unit which is so perceived is regarded as a composite of verbal and non-verbal behaviour (a 'behavioureme'), and *is* a unit in virtue of its 'purpose' or 'meaning'. It is structured into three 'complex overlapping components' or 'modes': the 'feature' mode (identificational features, some of which are naturally elusive and difficult to identify objectively), the 'manifestation' mode (physically realized substance), and the 'distribution' mode (dispersal among the rest of the units). Pike is therefore concerned with depth, breadth and height of focus in each of three modes. It is regrettable, in view of the overall unique value of his work, that he finds relatively little space (and, most uncharacteristically, very few further references) for the question of focus itself, although he attaches much importance to it.

There would seem to be two additional basic types of focus which we may term *conceptualization* and *expectation*. Informally speaking, conceptualization in the present context is taken to refer to what people *think* they do and ought to do, and what and how they think *about* what they (think they) do, allowing 'they' to be used reflexively or otherwise, and 'do' to refer to verbal as well as to non-verbal behaviour. Expectation concerns what people *expect* or *imagine* they will do (did, would do, would have done, etc.).

The fundamental relevance of a socio-linguistic approach to the speech event in terms of what and how (and how far) people think about what they do deserves some treatment. Conceptualization in this respect ranges from the intuitive, where in effect we cannot put what we are doing into words (or where the language —or language in general—has no appropriate and available means of expression) to the fully verbalized analytical (see W. W. and W. E. Lambert, 1964, p. 44 ff.; and J. S. Bruner, 1960, 1962). It can be correct or mistaken ('commands' mistaken for 'advice', etc.: see T. Burns, 1957). And it can possess or lack clarity of focus: what we and others do may be not so much mistaken as simply lost from sight, unattended to in the rush of events, as when we make efforts to explain ourselves better, strike an appropriate note of uncertainty or deference, verbally and nonverbally reinforce others when they speak, wait for cues, and engage in a thousand and one other such activities, as a rule taking little note at the time of what exactly we are doing. In this last connection, it has been said that with their very slow decision rates our minds do not normally register expectancies across very small stretches (G. A. Miller, 1962a, and refs. therein). Instead, the receiver tends to resort to delayed-action tactics in the face of the torrent of words coming at him every time he is spoken to, thereby dodging the effects of small but cumulative errors. It is a moot question how far (or whether) the receiver employs selective processing strategies for handling grammatical deep structures (see G. A. Miller, 1962b), semantic or pragmatic content, etc.

Across a longer stretch of time, processing consists among other things of adopting in a sense a somewhat more conscious strategy of necessary laziness or 'non-comittedness . . . storing the gist of many successive sentences perhaps rather "openly" till we see where we are being led', this being 'part of the condition of a proper attitude of anticipation' (A. McIntosh). The producer rather similarly in effect *plans* ahead (G. A. Miller *et al.*, 1960) choosing among alternative 'routes' to a 'destination', or, if one wishes, among alternative choices answering a given need. The routes or choices that are not selected, as J. Lyons (1963a, p. 25) points out, impart meaning to the one that is. Ranges of possible choice, allowing for all types of constraint, are often likely to be extremely wide in most normal language behaviour (a journey involving just ten calls can be made in more than three million different ways).

Both in the short and the long term producer and receiver appear to be engaged in very similar kinds of conceptualizing activity. This of course is fundamental to generative linguistic theory (the language user's 'competence' underlies both production and reception), but even in the present more informal context one can suggest several similarities. Neither, for example, attends to all parts of a total utterance or text, the producer rarely rehearsing what he is going to say (he trusts, interestingly enough, that somehow it will all work out), the receiver attending as it were to the 'gist' of the stored input at intervals (and over the long term listening or reading 'lazily' or non-committally). Both may of course err in registering what is actually intended, or even said ('Did I say that? Surely not!'). For both, meaning is largely a function of choice among permissible alternatives. Both are concerned to avoid enslavement to whatever immediately precedes. And both have the task of achieving some degree of empathy with the other's conceptualizing processes.

There can be little doubt that different people and groups of people have different ideas about language and its use, both in general and on particular occasions; are more, or less, aware of what is going on linguistically; handle what they hear or read in a more, or less, deliberate manner; and plan utterances differently. Factors of this sort characterize participants in the speech event, and so very largely characterize the speech event itself. Bernstein distinguishes 'codes' of a language according not only to their grammatical, lexical, and phonological characteristics but also, more fundamentally, according to certain formative attitudes to language and according to differences in the conceptualizing processes of language production and reception. As we have seen, Bernstein wishes (or at one time wished) to connect classes in society with the use of one or both of two codes (by the 'lower working class' and 'middle class' respectively), termed 'restricted' and 'elaborated'. The first of these has the primary function of serving as a set of 'social symbols', the second as a set of 'individuated symbols', the first being more _predictable_, fluent, repetitive, etc., the second more individually _planned_, hesitant, complex, etc. The working-class child is not normally spoken to by his parents in a grammatically complex manner reflecting and encouraging the use of complex reasoning. 'It is important to realize that the working-class boy's difficulties in ordering a sentence and connecting sentences . . . are alien to the way he perceives and reacts to his immediate environment. The total system of his perception, which results in a sensitivity to objects rather than to the structure of objects, applies equally to the structure of a sentence.' The educational problem may be the hardest to bear; the child from a poor background finds himself having in effect—however he does it—to translate (while learning the code of) his middle-class teacher's utterances. Scholastically, socially ('The attempt to substitute a different use of language . . . is an attempt to change . . . the very means by which he has been socialized': 1961a, p. 304), and affectively, he suffers as a direct consequence.

For the middle-class child 'a theoretical attitude is developed toward the structural possibilities of sentence organization' (1961a, p. 291). Now if this *is* indeed a marked characteristic of educated language use, it readily suggests a tendency towards the creation of utterances in the one social group, and *recall* in the other. The interesting alternative, in the light of modern generative theory, is not the former, but the latter: for how long and to what extent are the creative linguistic capacities of some people *not* set in motion? E. Haugen (1962) lays considerable emphasis on the pressures exerted on the child by his peers to conform to linguistic norms. How far do these amount to pressures to recall and how far (if so) are they offset by adult pressures not to conform in this way? Is there perhaps a critical age for the development of a habit one way or the other? A. Inkeles (1966) writes: 'We may eagerly await the second volume of *The Review of Child Development*, which is to give us a chapter on "Language Development and its Social Context". If we are to judge from advance reports on the studies of Martin Deutsch and Irving Taylor at the Institute for Developmental Studies, we may yet meet some surprises in discovering that it is not the number but the use of words that distinguishes the under-privileged child.' It would appear that a feature of this work is the assumption of a basic contrast between 'a conceptual mode of expression' and 'the motoric mode' (p. 271, fn. 7).

There is also possibly some indirect relevance to the general point being made here in a rather lengthy test which was given in 1963 by the writer to some fifty 'lower-working class' 10-year-olds in Edinburgh. Given a sentence-beginning, written on the blackboard, they had to get out their pens and 'finish off the sentence in as many different ways as you can', and quickly. This was done over a period of time, without rehearsal, for 35 items, yielding for analysis 25,000 sentences. Scores were allotted according to grammatical variation in the responses. Overall scores ranged very widely, two bright examinees of IQ 106 and 107 coming out top, as their teacher had expected. Some of the responses were ingenious, and would seem to have reflected, in slow motion, something of the perhaps unsuspected *planning* capacity of such pupils. It seemed, too, to be the case that grammatical resourcefulness was bound up with situational resourcefulness (see J. B. Pride, 1963).

Predictability is of course a function also of the receiver's ability to predict. One's natural intuition suggests that we do not simply store incoming information until points are reached when we make a 'decision' about it all. We also predict, although again what kinds of features we predict or try to predict is not at all certain—it may be, for instance, that we are relatively set to predict items which are to receive tonicity. It is difficult to experiment, since no informant can state what he *has* predicted or processed (after a delay), particularly since predictions are no doubt multiple. The poet, of course, and the lyric writer for the top twenty, and all of us at some time, consciously aim to set up predictions or expectancies in the receiver in order to confirm or deny them (or both), and we can work backwards, too, realizing, for instance, in retrospect that some earlier expected choice had been in fact improbable in the later event.

The process of expectation, one feels, is not wholly a behaviourist fabrication. It is true that not many would now identify with G. A. Miller's position in 1951, namely that 'Sequential grammatical habits can be discussed within the framework of an associative theory of verbal behaviour.' But there may yet be some truth in what lies behind the behaviourist psychologist's remark, quoted by K. S. Lashley (1951), that he 'had reached the stage where he could arise before an audience, turn his mouth loose, and go to sleep' (p. 184). As J. R. Firth (1937) put it, 'Whatever is said is a determining condition for what in any reasonal expectation may follow' (p. 94). He called this 'contextual elimination', affecting both producer and receiver alike. Unrehearsed talk, lecturing, etc., is full of wrong turnings induced by the immediately preceding co-text and by the direction taken by the ongoing situation. Introspection—which even here, where it is most difficult, may not be entirely without value—further suggests that even mid-word expectancies are set up in the receiver, since we are often surprised when they are not confirmed: it could of course be argued that this is some kind of hindsight at work, but it seems reasonable to assume that it is not. 'Well, I'm afraid it's—', even without the customary glance at one's watch, is normally more than enough, without completion. It is not surprising that very few investigations into relationships between predictability and ability to predict on the one hand and ability to comprehend on the other, according to social group, have been undertaken, in view of the methodological difficulties involved, yet there can be little doubt that the self-propelling power of language shapes the course of the speech event more than most observable environmental factors.

# 8 The Problem of Validity

Ours has been called an age 'riddled with abstractions, often inadequate to a stubbornly plural reality' (W. Walsh, 1964). The 'imponderabilia of everyday life' (or, as Sapir put it, the 'nooks and crannies of the real') are always there. One does not wish description to be merely a *mirror* reflecting all the detail but none of the structure, but at the same time a largely inductive approach will act as a safeguard against purely speculative model-building, in which, in a very real sense, the analyst can impose too much of *himself* on the data.

Main interest in parole tends to attract a predominantly inductive approach, in langue a predominantly deductive approach. But neither of these pairs should be regarded as irreconcilable alternatives. In fact of course it is not possible in any case to work wholly inductively or wholly deductively. There will always be something of both present, in whatever sort of equilibrium. The problem of deciding how much of each to accept or to aim for can be given various kinds of illustration. For example, taking a predominantly inductive case, in his study of 'components of social culture' relevant to the choice of personal pronoun in nineteenth-century Russian literature, P. Friedrich (1966) had to decide whether or not (or for how long) to postpone speculation about the more general operation of a much smaller set of components, in favour of the ten which to him seemed to emerge inductively from the observed 'facts'. Those he settled for were general enough: 'topic', 'context', 'age', 'generation', 'sex', 'kinship', 'dialect', 'group membership', 'jural and political authority', and 'emotional solidarity'. In discussion, it was suggested that he could just as effectively have operated with two only: 'power' and 'solidarity'. Friedrich countered: 'I prefer a large number of analytical distinctions that are only one or two steps from the data, as against only two categories that would require many intervening steps and subdivisions.' What he meant was that, for example, if the 'power' inherent in 'age' operates upon choice of pronoun in exactly the same way as the 'power' in 'jural and political authority', then but only then would nothing be lost by handling the larger concept 'power' without reference to the more specific categories. Identity of operation includes, of course, degrees of independence or inter-dependence which each category exhibits relative to others. Consider, for example, the trouble sometimes caused to the English speaker in having to weigh together the relative significance of factors of age, sex, seniority, length of acquaintanceship, physical setting, iden_ _ _ of others present, etc., when choosing the 'right' address form . . .

Although there is a great deal of difference between, on the one hand, starting with ten factors which have (so far as the analyst is able) been allowed to emerge *inductively* from the data, and subsequently in some way demonstrating and eliminating redundancies, and on the other *deductively* checking whether two more powerful and speculative factors work in practice, it is still, as suggested above, usually difficult to avoid doing both, and probably in some measure impossible. The unavoidable necessity for some reductionism is expressed by J. B. Casagrande (1963) in these terms: '. . . we still are left with the largely historical task of accounting for the particular phenomena of specific languages and cultures, but I would ask whence come the explanatory principles in terms of which these accountings are cast, and in the case of comparative studies, whence come the categories and concepts that permit valid comparison' (p. 291). The point he is making is that they do not, and cannot, all spring like magic from the ground to be examined. Some prior perspective is essential for analysis. It need not perhaps be more than temporary—in K. L. Pike's terminology, an 'etic' framework (D. H. Hymes: 'scaffolding') for the discovery of 'emic' contrasts —but the analyst has to bring something to the data, just as the infant in acquiring the language presumably does.

On the deductive side there is still, however, a distinction between what the analyst himself brings to the data and what his informant is allowed to bring. Casagrande goes on to refer to techniques which, in C. O. Frake's words (1962), aim to 'tap the cognitive world of one's informants', discovering those 'features of objects and events which they regard as significant for defining concepts, formulating propositions, and making decisions'. That is to say, what might otherwise be unwarranted and overly pre-conceived reductionism by the analyst is replaced by his discovery of what amounts to more intuitive reductionism on the part of the participant himself. The participant is not only closer to the data: he is regarded as *part of* the data.

It has been observed, however, that 'The attempt to elucidate the native speaker's cognitive awareness of the classifying principles underlying his folk taxonomy will involve . . . some knotty problems of cognitive psychology' (A. R. Diebold, 1964, p. 258). This may be so, but should still not deter one from recognizing some of the more important respects in which the language user himself exercises classificatory judgment of one sort or another. In other words, we have to admit this aspect of things as a basic part not only of the methodology of socio-linguistics, but also of its subject-matter. More than this, one is saying that the 'honourable, indispensable, and deeply ingrained' habit of discounting informants' pronouncements on his language can be very misleading if indulged in indiscriminately. H. M. Hoenigswald (1966) urges the renewed study of 'folk-linguistics', but repeatedly expresses its subject-matter as nothing more than 'elicited cant', 'impurities in the conditioning of subjects', 'clichés', 'shibboleths', 'esoteric interpretation', etc. There is admittedly no lack of evidence on this score. Expressed attitudes are often or even usually very much at variance with performance; Hoenigswald wishes to stimulate investigation into the question of 'how well the subject's judgments and opinions tally with the truth' (p. 19). The crux of the matter, however, is surely what is meant by 'the truth', what kind of truth it is one is after. For Hoenigswald the truth clearly implies objectively measurable information. But one might well ask how much information that is worth having *is* objectively measurable.

The very term 'language', if it is to be taken as 'a system of arbitrary vocal symbols by means of which a social group cooperates', requires specification for the term 'social group' itself, not least in respect of *subjective* 'reference group' membership. As W. J. H. Sprott (1958, p. 11) points out, a fundamental part of the notion of social group is consciousness of belonging: there *is* a group because 'we' think 'we' belong to it. Similarly, it is by no means a simple-minded view which says that a 'language' *is* a 'language' (or a 'dialect' *is* a 'dialect', etc.) because its speakers feel it to be so, or feel themselves to belong to the group that speaks it. Social consensus is crucial as a guide in identifying the object of one's analysis.

There are four main criteria for demarcating boundaries among languages and dialects: historical (or 'diachronic') development, contemporary (or 'synchronic') description, intelligibility, and social consensus. Each will tend to yield different answers. Moreover, one has to contend with continuous scales in each case. For example, one thinks of the village dialects in India which form 'a continuous chain from Sind to Assam, with mutual intelligibility between adjacent areas' (J. J. Gumperz, 1962, p. 83). The whole question must be admitted as beset with uncertainties: how does one weigh structural differences, qualitatively and quantitatively (see esp. J. J. Gumperz, 1961)? What again is intelligibility in any case? In the face of such complexities (which are multiplied in strict proportion to the number of theories concerning 'structure' that might happen to prevail) one ignores social consensus at one's peril. One might have cause to deplore its effects, but it must be recognized as a factor in its own right. Beliefs and attitudes (which are not quite the same thing, although often indiscriminately equated) powerfully affect not only where one language (dialect, etc.) ends and another begins but also the development of standard languages, vernaculars, creoles, pidgins, class dialects, varieties in diglossia, etc.

The assessment of underlying values and how they interact may be difficult enough under any circumstances, but 'objective' determination seems to be particularly elusive. As Fishman puts it: 'In general, the phenomenological validity of the "prestige" concept is so widespread (i.e. speakers so commonly regard their language as appropriately prestigeful for *their* purpose) and the objective determination of the concept so difficult that the former level may be a better one to investigate than the latter' (J. A. Fishman, 1966, p. 445, fn. 40). The necessity to find out what or how the participant himself thinks about things applies equally to the investigation of factors which prompt language learning, code-switching, and borrowing. In none of these respects, however, is it necessary to go to the other extreme and exclude the judgement of the analyst himself. He has at the very least to select the questions to ask, and these are bound to lead the informant to answer (and in effect to analyse) in the light of what he in turn sees as their general drift. Moreover, there is the question of how *representative* the informant might be of the particular social group in question, and this, too, demands some prior judgment on the part of the analyst (see W. H. Whiteley, 1966, p. 146). Ultimately what takes place is an interaction between personalities. As Sapir once cogently put it: 'The personality of the anthropologist and of the individual with whom he interacts must structure the method.'

Two examples will be given, the first only indirectly (yet relevantly) connected with choice of language. It concerns an enquiry by S. Silverman (1966) into prestige stratification in a central Italian community. His stated task was to illustrate one way of discovering the 'principles by which the bearers of particular cultures organize their universe and respond to it in culturally appropriate ways'. Silverman makes use of techniques whereby specially selected informants are made to sort progressively pairs of families known to them according to relative prestige ranks; also to attempt to specify what it is in each case that seems to prompt that particular sorting, in particular to reveal what further attributes would enable each given family to move up the prestige ladder. Ways of speaking were (not surprisingly) found to be one such marker. Silverman's informants were in effect pressed to reveal, even to formulate, systematic aspects of 'cultural competence' of which they themselves may initially have been relatively unaware.

The second example illustrates the value of largely subjective empathy on the part of the analyst in those cases where considered informant responses are out of the question. This concerns a functional analysis, exploratory enough, of the language of 3-year-old nursery school children in a one-hour natural play situations (recorded and observed unseen) carried out by an experienced teacher (Mrs J. Y. Tough, Institute of Education, University of Leeds) and the writer. A very recurrent functional distinction soon presented itself, between the *description* of objects (and the other participant) and their *manipulation*. The distinction seemed certainly to be there, yet was by no means matched by formal linguistic contrasts of an immediately obvious sort. The same principle applied, to a lesser degree, in the case of several other clearly significant and recurrent functions: the expression of certainty and uncertainty, anticipation and recollection, clarification, compatibilities and incompatibilities, dependence relations of one sort or another, sequence of actions, and so forth, in the immediate or reported or imagined situations, and addressed to the other child, to an object, or to the speaker himself.

This last example raises the question of the identity of the socio-linguist: is he best or normally identified as linguist, sociologist, anthropologist, or combinations of these, or what? It seems reasonable to look at any given investigation in terms of how, in its various phases, relatively more 'closed' or given factors are matched with a more 'open' or problematical set. It is the latter which stamps the direction of work as more sociological, or more linguistic, etc. For example, with an inductive approach a given body of linguistic data, if related to, say, sociological factors should to this extent (and it is a very large extent) be regarded as a sociological piece of work. Conversely, the inductive discovery of patterning within linguistic correlates of a set of given sociological observations would be an essentially linguistic operation. On the deductive side, a linguistic speculation or given set of categories once related to sociological variables takes on a sociological aspect; and the places of sociological and linguistic can, as before, be reversed. One might go so far as to suggest that in broadly inter-disciplinary work, such as this is, what one starts out from certainly need not be what one is primarily interested in. The opposite is far more likely, in fact, to be the case. The difficulty of course lies in the need to develop the grounds of a starting-point which falls largely *outside* one's own discipline. In practice, the study of language in its social and cultural contexts covers a range of activities extending from the basically linguistic to the basically non-linguistic; also, as we have seen, to the conceivable possibility of a 'second descriptive science comprising language, beside that of present linguistics proper' (D. Hymes, 1964a).

Of basically linguistic work the most obvious is perhaps that which investigates linguistic habits and abilities associated with given socio-regional groups, whether in terms of choice of language, dialect, or style. It might be added that also essentially linguistic are studies such as those of E. Stankiewicz (1964) into 'the linguistic devices which serve to signal the emotional attitude of the speaker', which have 'so far been insufficiently and unsystematically explored' (p. 266). This particular essay prompted A. S. Hayes (1964, p. 154 ff.) to argue for more attention to 'expressive language' (on which 'functions' are the starting-point against which to investigate 'linguistic correlates'), as against the study of 'para-language' (whose limits are 'operationally defined in terms of a closed linguistic system').

The identity of the analyst himself, his interests outside his own field, and the extent to which he is willing to collaborate with those in other disciplines, naturally matter a great deal. The value of linguistic correlates of, say, sociological categories is likely to be more limited (moreover *linguistically* so) if those categories have been put there by the linguist as linguist. A very notable quality in Malinowski's approach to language is precisely the degree of validity in its original non-linguistic premises. Malinowski's faithfulness to the particulars of the social and cultural environment in which language is used, led Firth, as we have seen, to criticize what for him was an excessively 'realist' approach, emphasizing—as Firth put it—the 'brute fact' or 'concrete situation' in which the utterance is 'directly embedded'. Even so, Firth, too, was concerned to paint a picture of persons and personalities in terms of their 'accumulation of social roles', and for *this* reason stated that 'Unity is the last concept that should be applied to language'. Firth had a live interest in sociology, the general impression left by his writings being a certain tendency towards deductive statement invaluably modified by natural curiosity in fields lying ostensibly outside linguistics.

Knitted into Firth's somewhat ambivalent perspective is his clear (and of course quite unexceptionable) injunction to utilize scrupulous descriptive linguistic techniques. One has to avoid 'loose linguistic sociology without formal accuracy' (J. R. Firth, 1935, p. 31). But he did not go so far as to require that the categories of context of situation should themselves be *determined by* formal linguistic analysis. This is the theoretical view of 'neo-Firthian' linguistics in this country, and has been most clearly articulated by M. A. K. Halliday (1961). Halliday splits 'context of situation' into 'context' *and* 'situation', the former comprising categories of the latter which are relevant to choice of language. It is of course where the contextual categories come from that ultimately matters most. All, from the most general ('register') downwards, are said to be defined *formally*— which is to say in terms of grammatical, lexical, phonological, and graphological contrasts. More particularly, contextual meaning is required to be 'logically dependent on formal meaning', the statement of the one to 'logically precede' that of the other (one might ponder the significance of Halliday's fn. 15, however). This is a view of linguistics which tends to place method before subject-matter. 'Logical' dependence on formal meaning simply entails over-dependence on the linguist's own direct perception of formal contrasts, in terms of his own particular descriptive theory, which itself is said to owe nothing to contrasts of a 'situational' kind. A register category such as 'tone' or 'patronizing and/or jocular' (J. Ellis, 1966a, p. 85) becomes part of the linguist's equipment because in looking directly at the forms of texts, he has perceived certain patterns which he then decides to label in this way. Accordingly, very elaborate grid systems, 'logically' derived from formal contrasts, can be placed over the world of experience, or 'situation'. It is said, for example, that for the linguist two otherwise discrete 'situations' are identical if their formal realizations are identical. But one can only reflect that such a case must surely be impossible to illustrate. Leaving aside the question of whether or not this is a behaviouristic view of language use, the question of identity is a wholly relative one: *how* similar must two texts be to be 'identical'?

The dependence of context on form appears then to come down to dependence on the linguist's own personal perception of formal contrast. But this in turn, one suspects, derives after all in large (but ambiguous) measure from his perception of situational contrasts in the first place. The starting-point for all schemes of register may very well be in part the linguist's *non-linguistic* view of the world. If this is so, then independence from other disciplines in this respect is likely to be a distinct drawback. There is little to be gained from M. Gregory's view (1967) that the linguist should beware of a 'failure of nerve' in the face of situational variety, and instead feel more free to 'make' situational facts. W. S. Allen's statement is quoted with approval: 'There are no facts in linguistics until the linguist has made them.' This may very well be true, but the real question is surely that of how independent the linguist is in his fact-making. Gregory goes on to state that the situational facts which interest him as linguist are those which have 'high potential contextual significance'; and the linguist's task is to study the 'fixed ways of coping with certain recurring situations'. The drift of his remarks, and the perspective of this last particular phrase, place main emphasis on the 'fixed ways' rather than on the 'recurring situations'. Making facts does not justify total independence for the discipline concerned in their making.

# 9   Inter-disciplinary Approaches

To say of any investigation or discussion that it is partly or largely non-linguistic does not in itself imply that it has little to do with language nor that it has little interest for linguists. Take for example the approach by J. Rubin (1962) to the question of bilingualism in Paraguay. Over half the population switch between Spanish and a vernacular language called Guarani. 'Code-switching' behaviour of this sort is the given linguistic ground for the investigation of sociological and psychological factors that might bear upon choice of one language or the other —such as, for example, socio-economic class, urban and rural locality, intimacy, power relationships, sex and so forth. A comparable range of factors, as we have seen, emerges from P. Friedrich's study of personal pronoun usage in nineteenth-century Russian literature, where again the initial data are defined linguistically while the findings are social-psychological. W. Labov (1963) notices a marked degree of centralization in the pronunciation of diphthongs among some of the native inhabitants of Martha's Vineyard. What were the pre-disposing factors? They, hence the study itself, take us into an intriguing politico-sociological exploration. All three studies could have gone the other way: what, for example, are some of the characteristic linguistic habits of teenagers in the Paraguayan countryside, of characters in a Russian novel, of fishermen in Martha's Vineyard? It will of course only be when *all* the facts are told that the two approaches will yield the same answer and bear the same complexion.

No less interesting, but from a different point of view, are those apparently non-linguistic undertakings that seem as if they ought, by virtue of their goals and subject matter, to contain a strong linguistic component—yet do not. Take, for example, the analysis by R. Brown and M. Ford (1961) of 'Address in American English'. This piece of work is unfortunately least explicit where it might have been most linguistic. The authors state: 'It is desirable to study social structure in everyday life, but much of the everyday behaviour that is governed by social dimensions is difficult to record' (p. 234). Instead they aim to infer aspects of social structure from their abstraction of speech patterns, in this case 'forms of address'. Their general approach is stated to be a 'sort of controlled induction' (p. 235).

The various phases of induction and deduction in Brown and Ford's study, and the various forms of informant analysis, are not easy to identify. For example, forms of address are said—without further explanation—to be 'reasonably well described by a single binary contrast: FN or TLN' (first name; title and last name). Now this is only a quasi-linguistic assumption, which ought rather to have been based on prior linguistic investigation into variable means for the expression of address, not merely in terms of name-selection but also in terms of other co-occurring formal features: 'good morning!', 'how are you getting on?', etc. From this point Brown and Ford's study matches in principle those of Rubin, Friedrich, and Labov. Correlations (with FN/TLN usage) of a socio-psychological nature are sought (oddly enough) initially and primarily in thirty-eight modern American plays. Factors such as degree of acquaintance, age, sex, occupational status, and so forth, all fairly predictable, emerge. But it is not apparent how they emerge: how deductive, for example, was their 'controlled' induction? The authors conclude that, as in the case of personal pronoun usage in many Indo-European languages, one might well detect the operation of the two pervasive scales of 'power' and 'solidarity'. And further, these are felt to be abstractly linked in that 'intimacy' is seen to co-occur with 'condescension', and 'distance' with 'deference' (the senior person can afford to be the more familiar . . .). This, they go on, may be a 'linguistic universal' (p. 239). What we have been saying, however, about the very attenuated nature of the selected forms of address strongly suggests that even if the investigation were largely inductive the authors might still be working towards sociological correlations based on somewhat arbitrary linguistic grounds; or at any rate of an unduly atomistic nature.

There are further reasons why the linguistic validity of this particular study is in doubt. Over the whole of America the uniformity of address usage it is suggested 'must be great' (p. 234). But an assumption of this sort must be wrong; identity has to be found, not imposed or assumed. 'Unity is the last concept that should be applied to language.' Three sets of supplementary data are used as 'checks' on the conclusions drawn from the plays: direct informant observation (within what terms of reference is again not clear) of usage in a Boston drafting firm, questionnaires for business executives at MIT, and tape-recordings of children talking in Kansas. The extreme heterogeneity and indeed vagueness of setting (geographical, social, physical, numbers present, fact and fiction, etc.) is matched by the variety of data-gathering techniques—not merely to the extent that these can be given unequivocally differing labels but, more significantly, in that the reader is left to guess what the informants were instructed to do, how far the authors themselves were busy illustrating a ready-made hypothesis with ready-made categories, and the extent to which the criterion throughout was *obligatory*, *habitual*, or *acceptable* usage. In other words, had Brown and Ford been at all linguistically inclined, they might have started from an unblinkered look at their everyday social function for language, that is to say address in all its manifestations; gone on to elicit relevant linguistic data from rationally selected informants; and then perhaps sought to infer those dimensions of social structure which seemed to be mirrored by patterning in the linguistic data. Looked at like this, their work would have been more or less equally linguistic and sociological, although no doubt finally sociological.

These authors were seeking to locate dimensions of social structure in the form of 'semantic rules' which might be universal. Their general aim is not entirely distinct from that of C. Osgood's 'semantic differential' investigations. Osgood attempts to locate

dimensions of 'subjective culture' in the form of 'common semantic factors' which might also be universal. It is instructive to
compare their methodologies. Osgood (1963) explores how
affective meaning systems vary across cultures, languages, and
'concepts'. He begins by selecting 100 concepts (in the shape of
words) which have been 'selected by linguists and anthropologists as being "culture-fair" and that have survived stringent
back-translation tests with bilinguals from all of the six language-
families represented'. One hundred high-school boys in each
country are made to respond to each concept with one 'qualifier
(adjectives in English)'. These are then ranked for frequency,
and compared—for each concept—across the various groups of
responding subjects (100 concepts times 100 subjects times 6
countries). The 50 top-ranking qualifiers are then associated with
each other by 6 fresh groups of 100 subjects and the results
factorized. Three well-defined factors (or clusters of responses)
emerge from this, and are given the labels 'evaluative', 'potency',
and 'activity' (exemplified respectively by 'good-bad', 'strong-
weak', and 'fast-slow'). These are found to be noticeably constant
across subjects but (perhaps not surprisingly) not so across
concepts. They are regarded in this sense as potential semantic
universals. Osgood's control over experimental variables is most
rigorous after the point at which the various 'concepts' are
chosen (why *words*, why *these* words, and why *qualifiers* in response?). Unlike Brown and Ford, Osgood is careful to elicit
information from comparable groups in a comparable manner,
and more general factors are arrived at with the use of explicitly
inductive procedures owing relatively little to pre-conceived
categorizations on the part of the analyst.

It is clear that not a few of the 'speech functions' which Firth
mentioned, and many which he did not mention, as entering
into our 'linguistic human nature' are now the province of social
psychology, but minus—in almost all cases—any involvement
with linguistics or even a linguistic perspective. Many pieces of
work stop short at precisely the point where linguistic description
seems crucially relevant. For example, much interest has been

centred on the discussion group interaction work of R. F. Bales and his associates, an acceptably detailed account of which is available in W. J. H. Sprott (1958). Bales is concerned with the possibly alternating attention of the seminar group, on the one hand to the appointed task area, and on the other to an inter-personal area where status factors operate. Suggestions, requests for opinions, agreement, disagreement, and the like, are regarded as open to either or both interpretations. But as Sprott points out, there is the difficulty for the observer-investigator of knowing which remarks should come under which categories. In other words, there is an absence of underlying studies (along with the development of appropriate methodologies) of, for example, how different social groups convey suggestions under particular conditions of status relationship. We have all asked ourselves, at some time or another, 'How do I put this to him? How does one get this sort of thing across?'—These are sub-vocal markers of widespread socio-linguistic phenomena, or problems. The relation between Bales' work and socio-linguistics is rather ana-logous to that between literary stylistics and socio-linguistics: there is a 'stylistics' of group discussion, conversation, etc., still awaiting development, long after Firth so clearly advocated its pursuit.

Another concern of sociologists (or better perhaps 'social psychologists': see W. J. H. Sprott, 1958, p. 19; and W. W. and W. E. Lambert, 1964, p. 2 ff.) in this general field is with the question of verbal reinforcement: 'uh-huh', 'I see', 'go on', 'I'm listening', 'yes', and so on. The relevant scholarly literature of social psychology makes interesting reading. Perhaps not sur-prisingly, it seems that one can change a speaker's preferred sentence structures by saying 'good' whenever a particular struc-ture appears (W. W. and W. E. Lambert, 1964, p. 75). How long would it take, like this, to make a speaker who thinks he is chatting away about nothing in particular, provide one with an account of his views on classical music? One can do it, apparently. Implicit in all this are more general questions of how patterns of verbal reinforcement, including the reinforcement of others by the very young, develop into more or less habitual verbal behaviour.

The converse activity of what one might call conversational opportunism does not appear to have attracted attention. Part of the listener's job, for instance, is to watch out for cues which might connect with what he wants to say anyway or serve as associational hints to say something he had not already intended to say. There are not only cues of this sort, of course, but also as it were take-over cues which in effect say to the listener, 'help me out', or, conversely, 'be quiet I want to keep talking'. The first type might include, to take a simple example, lexical items which will prompt the use, by the listener, of items from various associated lexical sets. The transition points between units of any sort are often more interesting than the units themselves, and in the case of conversation such points are only partially marked by change of speaker. The linguist, sociologist, etc., no less than anyone else, might very understandably wish to know what they are not doing when they find themselves unable to indulge fluently enough in forms of verbal repartee that are highly valued in their society. Among many others, this is a kind of problem implicit in Firth's statement that 'Neither linguists nor psychologists have begun the study of conversation; but it is here that we shall find the key to a better understanding of what language really is and how it works' (1935, p. 32).

Inter-disciplinary collaboration involves locating unsuspected problems and clarifying distantly suspected problems as much as, if not more than, taking ready-made problems to someone else for advice. But even the latter course involves a far-reaching choice between supposedly self-sufficient *borrowing* on the one hand and allowing oneself to be genuinely *influenced* by what one borrows on the other. Not many will adopt such a standpoint as that of G. A. Miller (1965) when he urges his fellow psychologists 'to propose and test performance models for a language user' and in so doing to rely on the linguist to give them 'a precise specification of what it is a language user is trying to use'. Earlier, in *Plans and the Structure of Behaviour* (1960), Miller (and his co-authors) had acknowledged that certain psychological assumptions would have to be radically modified in the light of recent advances in grammatical theory. This is an extreme example of basic theoretical influence, illustrating the point made by C. Lévi-Strauss (1958) that '. . . when an event of (some) importance takes place in one of the sciences of man, representatives of neighbouring disciplines are not only permitted but required to examine promptly its implications and its possible application to facts of another order'.

Such a degree of influence may very well be felt to endanger the autonomy of one's own discipline within its proper area of competence. Yet self-sufficient borrowing, as an alternative, is not normally possible. What happens of course is that a need is felt for information relevant to one's own problem but belonging more obviously to another discipline; but very often the nature of the available information is such as to preclude its direct integration into the framework of one's own discipline (see for example D. S. Boomer, 1964); so one is then prompted to restrict the range of questions that went into the formulation of one's original problem. The application of linguistics to the teaching of English as a native or foreign language is just such a case: educational problems can easily become formulated so as to fit in (and, by degrees, fit in with) linguistics. Many linguists feel that inter-disciplinary borrowing leads all too readily to processes of 'drifting into sociology', 'sliding into psychology' (both phrases from M. Gregory, 1967), or to even worse fates. The line between allowing oneself to be influenced by or merely to borrow from another discipline is always difficult to draw.

Methodological insight is naturally worth seeking. K. L. Pike (1956) expresses the need for a *single* methodology: 'An event comprised of both verbal and non-verbal activities . . . could not be analysed by the combination of a linguist and a non-linguistic anthropologist, since . . . any joint analysis by the two of them would merely be an aggregate of conclusions' (p. 59). D. Hymes (1964b) adopts in principle the same perspective, but perhaps the most fruitful (if admittedly general) perspective is that of J. Z. Young (1955). Young speaks of the distinct 'language' of each

discipline, in effect its favourite ways of talking about its phenomena and abstractions, *its* systems of 'metaphor' for *its* purposes.
The search for new insights can gain fresh impetus by talking
about one's own familiar problems as if they were someone else's,
asking questions like: is the brain (like) an electric circuit?
Suppose it were, then how would we talk about it? He writes:
'It seems that a science goes on finding out more and more detail
within one language system until new comparisons are introduced.' Looked at like this, scholarship advances from one
'rewarding analogy' to another; moreover, the search for
rewarding analogies and new language systems has in most cases,
he goes on, been carried out in the fields of other connected
(or conceivably connected) disciplines. But let it be stressed
again that methodological expertise, in this or any other sense, is
inseparable from and always subject to a clear view of goals and
subject matter.

# 10 Native-language Learning

The native language is acquired from the earliest years in context, more exactly in *perceived* context. Language is a prime means whereby the infant engages in the task of making sense of context, as everybody knows. It is all the more surprising therefore that very little thought indeed is currently being given to this matter. In contrast, psycho-linguistic investigation, with virtually no reference to social context, values, etc., is well established: see, for example, U. Bellugi and R. Brown (1964), F. Smith and G. A. Miller (1965), J. Lyons and R. J. Wales (1966). In the first of these collections a plea by D. Hymes for attention to the acquisition of social functions by the infant along with the bare forms of language passed totally unheeded in the published discussion. Abstracts of recent and current investigations such as those provided in *The Linguistic Reporter* (April, 1965) and IJAL (33, 1, 1967) paint much the same picture, without one single really clear exception among some fifty or so items.

There is need then for socio-linguistic investigation into such matters as: role relationship discriminations displayed in the language of 3- and 4-year-olds; the development of speech functions; attitudes of parents and nursery school teachers to what is appropriate and inappropriate in the infant's language and in their own linguistic 'handling' of infants (what is 'correct' or desirable, how and whether to correct verbal behaviour, how and how much to encourage verbal independence and/or play with words, etc.—in each case related to what is in fact practised); the development and nature of attitudes to language on the part of the child himself (particularly perhaps among those who have suffered a geographical and/or social transition of some sort—how early does sensitivity on this score reveal itself?); and so

forth. It is largely a question of 'applying' socio-linguistic
questions (that have perhaps already been thought of or looked
into in other quite different connections) to the situation of the
very young language learner.

Later stages of native-language learning have attracted, if
nothing else, a good deal of comment. Much of this is hyper-
critical. There is said to be abundant evidence of 'regrettably
low' standards of English attained even by school-leavers and
university entrants (*The Examining of English Language*, 1964,
p. 2), while students at the university have been said to suffer
from an 'appallingly low level of performance' (J. Small, 1964),
and, in prose work, to give their tutors an impression 'both of
awkward labour and of breathless rush' (G. S. Fraser, 1965).
The writer is not competent to pass judgment on all such statements, but certainly no one will easily overlook the repeatedly
expressed injunction by the authors of the Newsom Report
concerning native language teaching at the Junior Secondary
school level: 'They are not likely to persevere unless something
is done to lessen their greatest handicap—that inability to
express themselves which soon convinces them that they have
nothing to express. A double obligation rests upon the schools.
They have to provide the background of conversation and
exchange of information which an educated family offers, and
they have to coax their pupils to take part in it' (ch. 14,
and paras. 49, 50, 86–9, 247, 324, 329, 330, 346, 467, 468, 484,
485).

The proper assessment of standards and proficiency must be
related to both individual and social components of language use.
In the first case one stresses what Bernstein calls 'subjective
intent', or what A. McIntosh (1965) calls 'appropriacy', on the
other one attends to the pressure of social norms, or 'adequacy'.
It should be apparent that socio-linguistics is concerned with
both, and to this extent constitutes a body of on-going work
which is of central relevance (however it may be applied) to all
those concerned with native-language teaching. Very much less
relevant are those views of language as some kind of instrument

which is put to use, the use that is to say divorced from language itself. It is difficult to avoid some degree of metalinguistic ambiguity: the English language works with a very great deal of 'concretization' (as B. L. Whorf has demonstrated rather graphically), and it is natural to speak of 'the use of English' without necessarily intending any such divorce. Yet there are many who do wish to see a basic distinction of this sort. G. A. Miller (1965), for example, as we have seen, wishes the linguist to give the psychologist 'a precise specification of what it is a language user is trying to use'. One often hears teachers, too, of very different persuasions, agreeing in principle that, to quote one, 'there is no point at all in showing children how to use language unless they have some language to use'. Perhaps the crudest expression (happily dying out in examinations and the classroom alike) is the time-honoured ritual of grammatical analysis. This has been referred to, in some of its classroom manifestations, as 'a kind of mumbo-jumbo about as remote from linguistic practice as anything could well be' (A. McIntosh, 1963, p. 119), awkward labours characteristically spent on short stretches of concocted language well within the repertoire of the normal 6-year-old. Perhaps it is no longer necessary to pronounce against such practices, illustrating as they do an extreme form of prescriptivism where 'right' and 'wrong' prevail and 'error'-spotting is the main object of the exercise.

Proponents of transformative-generative theory tend to express considerable doubt as to whether or not linguistics and psychology have very much to say that is relevant to problems in language teaching. N. Chomsky (1966), for example, speaks for many others in asserting: 'I am, frankly, rather sceptical about the significance, for the teaching of languages, of such insights and understanding as have been attained in linguistics and psychology' (p. 43). He goes on to point out that these disciplines are 'in a state of flux and agitation'; he himself believes they should shake themselves free from what he refers to as the 'myth' that linguistic behaviour is 'habitual' and that a fixed stock of 'patterns' is acquired through practice and used as the basis for 'analogy' (p. 44). Teachers, he says, 'have a responsibility to make sure that ideas and proposals are evaluated on their merits' (p. 45). What this amounts to is that (*a*) language and the use of language are distinct, (*b*) linguistics (concerned only with language) is largely irrelevant to the needs of the language teacher—who is concerned with use, and (*c*) the study of language in context is inherently valueless 'it is only under exceptional and quite uninteresting circumstances that one can seriously consider how "situational context" determines what is said, even in probabilistic terms' (p. 46). A main object of the present account, however, has been to show that the interests of the socio-linguist are by no means so behaviouristic.

Socio-linguistics is very much concerned to ask what kinds of teaching practices seem on the face of it to be most in sympathy with its own perspectives. There would appear to be two closely related principles which it would naturally support. First is the recognition that even though the teacher certainly has the task of leading the pupil to greater mastery of the native language in new directions, a still more important factor is that of the pupil's own inner motivation. Loss of contact is a greater danger than loss of direction. In this light, the English teacher's task, perhaps above all else (and certainly with the type of pupil whose needs are discussed in the Newsom Report), is that of acquiring and exercising a 'sense of touch' (W. Walsh, 1964, ch. 1), a 'linguistic tact' which balances the need for 'sympathetic projection' against the needs of the theme of the lesson.

Firth's statement that it is in the study of conversation that 'we shall find the key to a better understanding of what language really is and how it works' should warn us that conversation is not simple; it is not easy, or necessarily easy to *achieve* conversation. To take one (and it is only one) aspect, for example, it may be supposed that there are features in the language of the teacher, the way he encourages, checks, agrees, disagrees, changes the subject, expresses surprise, shows amusement, supplies information, and so on, perhaps, too, the way he reveals to his pupils what his attitudes are to their language, that help to make for success or failure in this respect. There is a sense in which his handling of language affects the situation not as a mere adjunct to more powerful factors of personality but as ingredients *of* personality: 'linguistic human nature' embodied in the teacher himself. There seems no necessary reason, in principle, why it should not be possible to predict about certain aspects of the language of this or that teacher that his pupils are that much more, or less, likely to make certain types of linguistic response— or to respond at all.

In this general connection the socio-linguist would wish to sound a caution against over-regard for 'topic'. 'Centres of interest', for example, in writing as in speaking or reading, are not necessarily best reduced to or elicited in terms of 'topics': the analysis of writing interests might just as profitably be undertaken in terms of role relations, speech functions, attitudes, etc., recognizing that each such category admits of very considerable refinement. The title of a writing assignment may indeed be the only *immediate* stimulus for interest, but will surely not in itself generate whatever *subsequent* interest the pupil might come to feel as the business of writing gets under way. The complexity of motivations which enter into the writing of compositions explains why it was possible to point out in the compendious review of research into written composition in schools in the United States which was edited by R. Braddock *et al.* (1963) that very little was then known about the question of writing interests, nor even about how to set about investigating the matter.

There may be another reason why 'topic' might well, as it were, be played down in the context of the English lesson. This is, of course, that English is not basically a 'content' subject at all. J. S. Bruner (1960) argues that any 'idea' can be represented 'honestly and usefully' in the thought forms of children of school age. In the same volume, a teacher of mathematics at the University of Illinois states about the introduction of set theory to quite junior classes in the school: 'It may be that nothing is intrinsically difficult. We just have to wait until the proper point of view and corresponding language for presenting it are revealed.' This is a perspective that in effect (and no doubt with justice *outside* the English classroom) sees the teacher as *translator*, determined to get 'what' he wants to say 'across' to his pupils. One can only suggest, however, that the kind of language that belongs to the English lesson is of a different kind, much more a form of activity that can originate from and be given direction by the pupils themselves; as Barth might put it, a place where transactional speech events can give expression to and modify personal and social values. J. N. Britton (1965) writes: 'Those experiences which are not areas of common knowledge are the area of the English lesson'; more than this, he believes that even if we *are* (as indeed we must be) interested in the 'impersonal' uses of language, there is still the very real danger of trying to teach such language, too prematurely; that instead one should see this kind of ability as 'a development from the personal language'. The distinction that Britton is making is that which informs much of what Sapir wrote, between language as 'communication' and language as 'communion'. The English lesson should be a place where mere talk is valued.

The second basic principle is that the learner should be involved in a largely inductive approach to the subject which admits at the same time of a good deal of 'intuitive' as opposed to 'analytical' learning. Much thought has been given to the intuitive learning of subjects like mathematics. If intuitive learning in this particular field does provide the best foundation for later analytic learning, and if the teacher's task is so to arrange things that intuitive learning at early stages is allowed to develop naturally and yet purposefully into analytic learning, without loss of intuitive ability, then there is every reason why one should be thinking along these lines in the field of native-language teaching. Unwillingness on the part of the teacher to project his own analytic knowledge into the intuitive mode of the young learner can do much damage. A too premature formalism has the effect of making the pupil believe that he has yet to learn something which in a sense he already knows, with the consequent danger of warping the pupil's intuitive powers. The fortunate child is encouraged to play with numbers long before he is expected to put what he is doing into words. It is now widely believed that the 10-year-old child can handle, if not put into words, the operations of what one authority has termed 'a formidable amount of highbrow mathematics'. In more general terms it has been said that intuition is founded on 'a combinatorial playfulness that is only possible when the consequences of error are not over-powering or sinful' (J. S. Bruner, 1962). Knowledge about language, too, should presumably therefore be rooted in an environment which allows what the child feels to be 'free' play with words—even if this is what the teacher knows to be 'controlled' play. What is more, every transition from intuitive to analytical activity should, if possible, follow from evidence of readiness in the part of the particular pupils. And it is infinitively better, one imagines, to make such transitions too late than too early.

To what extent should socio-linguistic perspectives have effect upon the development of in-service courses for teachers and administrators, undergraduate courses, and classroom teaching itself? This question will be answered very briefly, and with particular reference to courses which enter into the education of prospective teachers. The writer is convinced that a substantial proportion of all such work should be of this nature, especially in the early stages; that sensitivity to the character of one's own and others' performance, spoken and written—which should undoubtedly in any case be developed continuously throughout any such course—is of its nature largely socio-linguistic; that the student's appreciation of the nature of attitudes to language and language users is well developed by reference not only to the native context but also to settings much further afield; and that in general syllabuses should be more than usually responsive to what the particular students themselves bring to them.

# 11 Second-language Learning

The question of whether, and how, linguistics might be 'applied' to problems of second-language teaching is now a very familiar one. But there is reason to believe that the sheer urgency of the problem has distracted attention from the value that might accrue from enquiries into processes of second-language *learning*.

Some of the opening remarks of D. E. Broadbent (1967), on the state of current knowledge concerning the psychology of modern language learning, provide a useful framework for a socio-linguistic approach to the problem:

(*a*) 'There is very little indeed that has been published directly in this area using the methods and criteria of academic psychology.

(*b*) There is a very large amount of expertise and opinion-based activity amongst language teachers, which is based on assumptions about human behaviour and which seems to work. It would not, however, come up to the scientific standards of a purist psychologist.

(*c*) There are a large number of areas of general psychology which are of relevance, but the full implications have not been worked out in the special situation of language learning.'

In (*a*) and (*c*) here one might quite adequately replace 'psychology' by 'socio-linguistics'. In (*b*), however, if one had so to generalize, it would be necessary to acknowledge some degree of failure on the part of language teachers in general to recognize the very basic relevance of the learner's socio-linguistic environment, behaviour, motivations, attitudes, and so on. Considerations of this sort may loom large enough in the teacher's experience, yet somehow still manage to strike him as peripheral, in the sense that language continues to be seen as some kind of sum total of grammatical, phonological and lexical systems largely independent of social function. Trends in second language teaching have long followed, and will continue to follow, trends in the academic study of language; socio-linguistics, being relatively new on the scene, has not yet made much of an impact on teachers and textbooks.

'Situational' approaches to language teaching derive much of their undoubted impetus and value from *psychological* 'assumptions about human behaviour', rather than from the conviction that what is learned is shaped and coloured to a marked degree by underlying socio-linguistic factors. To put the matter another way, it must be very common experience for the second-language teacher to feel that he is imposing, through the instrumentation of textbooks, syllabuses, examinations, etc., a kind of language and kinds of skill which are quite alien to the social needs of his pupils; but is it equally commonly felt that sympathy for their needs, interest in their interests, and personally acquired information about their general environment, would gain much from the insight that might stem from disciplined studies of the place of language in their lives? Every language teacher knows how encouraging the generative nature of language learning can be on those occasions when motivation to communicate is at its highest. If Chomsky is right to doubt the basically 'habitual' and analogical nature of linguistic behaviour, and if at the same time generative linguistics is still very far from achieving a 'level of theoretical understanding that might enable it to support a "technology" of language teaching' (N. Chomsky, 1966, p. 43), then there seems all the more reason to develop syllabuses in the light of a proper understanding of some of the socio-linguistic dynamics of learning situations.

One of the first requirements for sound language teaching is for adequate socio-linguistic descriptions of those features of speech communities that bear most heavily on the needs and motivations of the particular learners concerned. Taking some of these quite at random, since one hopes there is very little in the present account that is necessarily irrelevant to any given case, one might consider, for example: the degree to which the community itself, or some part of it, is monolingual, bilingual, multilingual, diglossic, etc., and the relation of such facts to the facts of individual bilingualism and linguistic exposure; modes of use (production, reception, inner speech); channels of communication; identities of regional and social groups characterized by habitual choice of language; 'domains' of use in terms of physical settings and, more importantly, role relationships; speech functions; attitudes towards and motivations for learning languages, dialects, and varieties, and towards habits of bilingualism and bi-dialectalism; the nature and effects of language planning (as, for example, choice of media of instruction in schools and higher education, adoption or modification of writing systems, deliberate hastening of lexical expansion: see E. Haugen, 1966b, for a general discussion); the nature and extent of socio-cultural adaptation suffered by languages and dialects in contact, not least by second-languages in school curricula (including emphases of this nature lent to a second language by teachers of it who happen to be native speakers of—for the learners—some other second language); and so forth.

Each of these factors, and many more, can be regarded in terms of *statistics* (speakers, languages, geographical extent and density and distribution, etc.); *beliefs* entertained by various groups of persons (concerning others as well as themselves); directions of *change*; levels of *proficiency* (involving questions such as the nature of intelligibility—reciprocal and non-reciprocal, of 'compound' and 'coordinate' bilingualism, etc.); *inter-relationships* among the various factors (including incompatibilities—as between skills taught in schools and those used or valued or needed in the community outside the school); how each factor not only inter-relates with others but also assumes greater or lesser *relevance* or power to override the effects of others; the appropriateness or otherwise of different *methodologies* for analysis (notably involving choice between the use of introspection and observation, artificial and naturalistic settings: see esp. S. Ervin-Tripp, 1964); and finally, the extents to which behaviours, attitudes, beliefs, etc., are—or are held to be—*appropriate, normal,* and *obligatory.*

A large number of quite distinct types of investigation could be sketched out drawing on different combinations of all such factors at various levels of refinement. To what extent it would be possible to generalize, as J. B. Carroll (1962) would wish to do, among 'language learning situations' with the use that is to say of certain 'key variables' (p. 75), and excluding all others, is a moot point. Carroll wishes to 'make predictions concerning the characteristics and course of the learning process' in each type of situation, assuming that each can be 'discovered to have numerous analogues' (p. 76). But in order to stand a real chance of finding analogues to a situation such as 'native American children learning French in American public schools', and extending as widely as 'many classrooms of countries in the British Commonwealth (U.K., Canada, Australia), in West European countries, and in certain parts of the USSR' (p. 76), one's key variables would have to be very general indeed: yielding, it would seem, equally general predictions.

Each of Carroll's key variables is indeed very general. 'Degrees of difference between languages', historically derived, are specified as precisely five in number, and concern the sound system, grammar, vocabulary and writing system, without reference to socio-linguistic considerations. Yet socio-linguistics should be recognized here again as centrally relevant. How is one to compare say two grammatical systems except by reference in each case to what J. Ellis (1966b, p. 150) terms 'some tertium quid comparationis'? Socio-linguistics is the name for the study of just such a basis for comparability—comparability also implying translateability. Languages are, moreover, best compared not only as wholes but also, or perhaps preferably, as parts. For example, even with presently available information, it would be highly instructive to compare the personal pronoun systems of many seemingly quite different languages. Quite a number of paired comparisons already exist. J. C. Catford (1965, p. 45) illustrates the different contextual and structural values of personal pronoun forms in Bahasa, Indonesia and English.

The former gives morphological expression to distinctions between 'exclusive' and 'inclusive' reference, and between 'familiar' and 'non-familiar' relationships; English but not Indonesian has gender distinctions; and so forth. French, Italian, etc., match Indonesian more closely than does English in the second person (tu, vous); and more generally, there are many languages which also obligatorily convey an exclusive/inclusive distinction somewhere in the morphology of the pronoun, verb, etc. Again, there are no doubt many differences between Standard Korean, Bahasa Indonesia, and French. The obligatory expression in Korean, however, of an 'in-group'/'out-group' distinction, in its choice of verb suffixes for address (see S. E. Martin, 1964, p. 409), is relateable in kind to Indonesian and French pronoun usage.

Even when this is recognized, however, its relevance to the learning situation itself will still vary enormously with another of Carroll's variables: 'the skill of the teacher in the second language and in teaching it'. But what precisely (or even generally) is implied by the term 'skill'? This appears to be the only 'key variable' that could be made to connect even remotely with the question (otherwise ignored) of *what* aspects of the L2 are in fact taught—rather as if this were some kind of constant across all the situational analogues from Canada to the USSR. 'Level of attainment expected' (p. 73) also begs this and other equally large number of questions; it may be true to say of American children learning French in American public schools that 'it is expected that each child will progress as far as he can toward full competence in all aspects of French' (p. 75), but what do 'full competence' and 'all aspects' mean? It is notable that Carroll's other two hypothetical examples of types of situation duplicate this requirement, rather than elucidate it contrastively. In some respects, on the other hand, Carroll multiplies distinctions in an equally imprecise manner. What, for example, is gained by asserting a categorical distinction between 'positive', 'neutral', and 'negative' motivation? What is the nature of 'intrinsic' as compared with 'extrinsic' motivation? If intrinsic motivation 'has to do with the child's own attitudes towards the learning of the language', extrinsic motivation with the 'rewards or punishment which emanate from others', then one still has to identify the distinguishing characteristics of each type of motivation for each particular setting—and thereby, quite possibly, blur the distinction itself.

Even more important, however, is the question of what Carroll chooses to omit entirely from his list of key variables: for example, the uses to which it is expected the learner will put his knowledge of the L2 after leaving school (who uses what language with whom and when . . .), how far the learner and his teachers know what these are; the extent to which the learner will be required later on to switch codes according to the play of one contextual factor or another—and, more immediately, the nature of the code-switching habits forced on him by the school curriculum in conjunction with the out-of-school environment; the extent to which and respects in which the pupil can be observed to pick up the L2 outside the school, and how far these natural processes of language learning are taken into account or even envisaged by teachers, textbooks, administrators, etc. ('degree of contact with the L2', one of Carroll's variables, sub-categorized into four cases, does not in itself connect with the question of what the pupil makes of the various situations in which he might stand a chance of learning something); the amount and direction of socio-cultural adaptation suffered by the L2 (at the hands of native speakers of the learner's L1, or of the L2 itself, or of some third language), how this factor relates to levels of achievement of one sort or another, and the manner in which the L2 is adapted to meet problems presented by extreme sociocultural heterogeneity among pupils in the same school or class; and so forth. No doubt these particular questions could easily be supplemented by others. The real point, however, is that each such question is not necessarily to be answered by reference to some fixed set of cardinal points or 'cases'.

Most of the really significant questions are rather too open, and contain too many variables, for any such global comparison to be really useful. Take, for example, the place of vernacular languages in the school curriculum (a useful discussion of which is that of W. E. Bull, 1955), and in particular the place of pidgins. R. A. Hall jr. (1965) describes pidgins as 'the very first stage of rudimentary language learning' (p. 127), more drastically reduced in grammatical and lexical shape (often in terms of number, case, gender, etc.) than supplemented (with, for example, aspect markers which may trace from 'sub-stratum' languages). Creoles are simply pidgins which have been promoted to the role of native languages for sizeable groups of people. Hall claims that Neo-Melanesian pidgin has been found adequate for Europeans to discuss with each other such subjects as theology and international law. However, the descriptive statements about pidgins and creoles which are provided, and any familiarity at all with texts in these languages, does not so easily bear out his optimism. The sentence-structures of pidgin tend to be relatively simple, with, for example, much co-ordination, while subordinating conjunctions are rare. But if items like 'because' *are* rare, then there would seem to be that much less functional power attaching to these languages. Similarly, if vocabulary is reduced in the sense that the range of meaning of many items tend to be unusually wide, then one is thereby uncomfortably reminded of the lexical pitfalls of Basic English. A great deal of metaphor (bearing, incidentally, some considerable likeness to literary Anglo-Saxon!) of the 'grass of the head/face/mouth' variety can be poetic and amusing—owing much to the rough humour of traders—yet fail to cover up a well-nigh crippling absence of lexical refinement. Yet Hall still considers that since, as in New Guinea, pidgins are sometimes essential as a lingua franca among non-Europeans, more use should be made of them in the educational system. 'It cannot be said that one language is intrinsically inferior or superior to another; and it is universally recognized that learning should begin in the child's mother tongue' (p. 141). Hence the teaching of arithmetic in pidgin in New Guinea is claimed to be preferable to using English: 'you have to be sure what you mean and say it clearly, in which case there is no danger of being misunderstood.

Pidgin has no big empty words or abstract nouns like "multiplica-
tion" or "division" which the native learner can use grandiosely
without knowing what they mean. Talking Neo-Melanesian in
class forces both teacher and pupils to talk sense' (p. 145).

These comments require some rejoinder, and on various levels.
First, there is a difference between being forced to 'talk sense'
and being forced to try to talk sense. Second, one must not
condemn a language (English in this case) merely because one
has seen it badly taught: there is plenty of evidence for the
possible effectiveness of the teaching of all subjects in the curriculum at a very early stage through the medium of a second
language (see H. H. Stern, 1962, esp. references to G. E. Perren
therein; and W. E. Bull, 1955, referred to above; note that
Stern's is a UNESCO publication, post-dating UNESCO, 1953,
which Hall commends on this issue, by ten years). Third, the
sense of Sapir's compelling statement 'when it comes to linguistic
form, Plato walks with the Macedonian swineherd, Confucius
with the head-hunting savage of Assam' is surely that in the
course of time and in very favourable circumstances a 'little
language' (Hall's apt expression for pidgins) *can* become a big
language: there is nothing in its structure to prevent this happening. But languages are not enriched overnight. Talking sense in
pidgin, one would have thought, means talking sense only up to
a certain point in a large number of domains, particularly the
scientific.

Even so, much depends, as always, on the particular setting.
Pidgins as well as creoles and all small vernacular languages
possess their own special strengths, those of pidgins proving their
origins in the 'successive and reciprocal imitations' of particularly
urgent but restricted needs for communication (see *Anthropological Linguistics*, 6, 7, 1964, esp. p. 20 ff., on Hawaiian pidgin
English). Pidgins may or may not find a rightful place in some
particular educational curriculum, but not surely on the grounds
of any sweeping formula.

Needless to say the study of socio-linguistic factors affecting
the learning situation can be conducted by other than survey

techniques reflecting the status quo. It may sometimes be more instructive to initiate something and see what happens, as was done quite notably by G. E. Perren (1959a, 1959b, 1960) in the early stages of the Nairobi Special Centre English-medium 'Peak' Course. In aiming to establish an explicitly educational element in the selection and grading of teaching material it was felt necessary, among other things, to pay very particular regard to the social environment of its young learners. Much, too, can be gathered directly from the use of adult or near-adult learners of an L2 as, in effect, informants. The teacher who speaks the L2 natively and who is enabled to set aside textbooks and syllabus requirements for a reasonable period of time, and who is fortunate enough to possess a tape-recorder and find it welcomed in the classroom, can elicit much valuable information. The mutual benefit to be gained from focusing many or even most lessons on the very natural desire among the learners themselves to give expression to their own cultural heritage soon becomes evident. Such an aim can be achieved of course not only by bluntly asking for this type of information but also by inviting it to assert itself through the introduction of imaginary situations or even informal games.

The problem of what to tell the learner (as well as the teacher) *about* the language being learned is also important. D. E. Broadbent (1967) points out that the current tendency to minimize teaching of an abstract knowledge of the L2 may not take sufficient account of the extent to which the learning of a principle will transfer to a new situation. He goes on: 'To take an analogy, it is necessary for a pilot to learn the fine muscular movements of flying an aircraft . . . It is also useful, however, for him to understand the principles of aerodynamics so that he is not surprised to stall in a high-speed turn, and it is essential for him to understand the principles of navigation rather than to be taught the way to each new city by practising specifically on that route' (p. 9). Broadbent's general point lends support to the view that the second-language learner will benefit not a little from instruction in the nature of language, and of his task as a language learner. Moreover, this would entail explanation of language learning as the making of discriminations that are not purely grammatical, phonological, lexical, etc., but also (or rather) socio-linguistic. Further than this, he should be made more aware than he might already be of certain aspects of the roles played by the L1 and L2 in his own community. The question is not so much that of *whether* principles should be taught explicitly, as of *what* principles should be taught.

Different processes of language learning result not only in a contrast between compound and co-ordinate bilingualism, but also in different shades of compound bilingualism, depending on the nature of the existing knowledge to which new learning is assimilated. (Broadly speaking, compound bilingualism involves some degree of conscious translation in the speaker's mind, whereas co-ordinate bilingualism does not: see H. H. Stern (1962) for a useful introduction to this subject.) As D. E. Broadbent (1967) points out: 'Some of the contemporary approaches produced by educationists appear to be aiming deliberately at the production of the co-ordinate type, while naturally occurring bilinguals are quite often of the compound type. It is not at all clear what the advantages are in each case' (p. 5). It may be worth looking further therefore into the possibilities inherent in socio-linguistic explanation, to the learner, of language and second language teaching material and the problems it presents with a view to assisting him in developing a beneficial form of compound bilingualism. Learner and teacher alike are bound in any case to conceptualize their task in some degree. The language lesson itself is a speech event in its own right, in which all concerned are therefore engaged, at various levels of awareness, in focusing on one aspect or another of meaning. The kind of psychological and linguistic insight which sees language learning as more than the development of 'basic perceptual and motor skills', more that is than the unthinking and uncreative activation of specific responses to specific stimuli, is by no means incompatible with the development of socio-linguistic perspectives.

There are two main educational fields to consider—the school system inside Somalia, on the one hand, and the experience of school-leavers studying overseas, on the other. The language patterns of school curricula in the north of the country differ markedly from those in the south. To quote a small extract from the Report ('Somalia', 1965): 'In the north, a child first passes through a Koranic school where the medium of his instruction becomes modern colloquial Arabic, and where he becomes acquainted with the Classical Arabic of the Koran. Some time before he is 10 years old (in rural areas this may be between 10 and 14) he moves on to an Elementary School, where Arabic continues to fulfil this role as medium of instruction. At this point, English is being taught as a subject. At the Intermediate stage, English assumes this medium function, and retains it throughout the Secondary School. Arabic, meanwhile, is taught in the Intermediate and Secondary Schools as a subject language; at Sheikh Secondary School it takes up nearly 13 per cent of the total curriculum time. In the south, Arabic is used as the medium of instruction in the first two grades of the Elementary School after which—at present—Italian assumes this function. English was introduced in the Academic Year 1963/64 in Grade 3 of the Elementary School as a further second language, alongside Arabic. It is intended to replace Italian as the medium of instruction in Grades 3 and 4 by Arabic in the near future. Italian is currently the medium of instruction in the Intermediate Schools, while in the Secondary Schools in the south there are three media, depending on the school—Italian, Arabic and English. It is intended that, ultimately, as in the north, English will become the medium of instruction in the Intermediate Schools in place of Italian, but no final decision has yet been taken with respect to these or to the Secondary Schools.'

The Report goes on: 'There are at least two major aspects of this situation to be noted. *First*, the output from the schools is composed of multilingual individuals with varying competence in each of several languages. As it stands, this situation does not easily lend itself to single medium teaching at any further institution of learning. *Second*, as the three members of the Unesco 1962 Educational Planning Group remarked, the curriculum "stresses the linguistic side of education too strongly". This second point is certainly so. In Elementary Schools in the south, 50 per cent of the pupils' time is spent learning Arabic and Italian—against a home background of Somali.'

At the school-leaving level, the facts state that over 500 students were studying 26 subjects in 17 overseas countries (representing at least 12 different native languages) at the degree level, while more than 500 others were following 12 very distinct types of course in 13 overseas countries (in at least 10 languages). Such students, as a group, will be possessed of fluent abilities in many different languages, more than half of which play no normal part in Somali life. That is to say, translation (in fields where translation may be particularly difficult) necessarily takes on what can only be imagined as survival value for many of the most highly educated members of society. Moreover, in the case of those languages which *are* used in Somalia, overseas students are bound to bring back with them varieties more in keeping with each particular overseas environment than with that of Somali life itself. The real strength of an international language, it should be remembered, is quite largely a function of its power and adaptation to national or otherwise local environments; and this entails certain advantages attaching to their being learnt locally.

Status, power, and solidarity are hard at work in discriminating among the three main outside languages in Somalia. Arabic draws much of its strength from the fact that Somalis are Moslems. In some schools at least the English lesson provides merely another vehicle for the teaching of the Koran—through the use of translation. Arabic is in many respects the language of prestige, *par excellence*. Italian, however, is the predominant language of commerce and (slightly less so, beside Arabic) law: one does very nearly all one's shopping in Italian. English, on the other hand, is the language overwhelmingly used by United Nations personnel, by many overseas delegations, and so forth. The ever-present underlying tension between Arabic and English (and to a lesser extent Italian) is painfully obvious in respect of the long-standing but still unresolved and extremely delicate problem of whether to develop an Arabic or a Roman script for Somali: the Somali government were not necessarily prepared in 1964 to accept any outside linguistic advice. Somali itself has the strength and weakness of any other vernacular, and being unwritten into the bargain ('When a road accident occurs, the police will question witnesses in Somali, but write their report in Italian in the south, or English in the north . . .': Andrzejewski, 1962, p. 177), would seem to be a rather weak candidate for official status, or indeed for additional strengthening beyond a certain stage in the educational curriculum; yet at the same time it must not be forgotten that it is the sole vehicle for much that identifies the Somali as what he is.

Here are a few details from the Report, as for December 1964:

(i) At the *Egyptian Secondary School*, Mogadiscio, all subjects are taught through the medium of Arabic, textbooks being supplied from the United Arab Republic. Syllabuses in use are as those in the UAR. From the first year English is taught as the 'first European language'; at the beginning of the second year, if he is to be a specialist in literary studies, the pupil may also choose French or Italian.

(ii) The *Secondary School*, Mogadiscio, put up under bilateral aid from the USSR, and opened in September, 1964, has established a provisional curriculum which allows for all instruction to be given in English, for a relatively substantial amount of tuition in the Russian language and literature, less time for the Arabic language, and no time for Italian. Somali teachers (who numbered, in December, 1964, four, alongside ten Russians) teach English and Arabic.

(iii) In the *National Teacher Education Centre*, Afgoi, English is being used as the medium of instruction. The pupils' knowledge of English has previously been built up over four years of Intermediate schooling in the north; all speak Arabic and Somali, a few speak Italian. The syllabus for the first year, largely developed by American staff in the first instance (prior to the expected assumption of responsibility by Somali staff), allows for five periods per week of each of English and Arabic (alongside other subjects).

(iv) At the *Scuola Magistrale*, Mogadiscio, Italian is the medium of instruction for all subjects. Arabic and English (since 1962) are taught as subjects, by Somali teachers.

(v) The *Scuola Media Superiore*, Mogadiscio, about half of whose graduates currently pursue university courses in Italy, teaches through Italian, and finds an equal place for English and Arabic as subjects throughout its four years (that is, about 10 per cent of the total curriculum time is given for each).

(vi) The *Istituto Tecnico per Ragionieri*, Mogadiscio, also teaches through Italian, and conducts the same number of Arabic and English classes each week as the Scuola Media Superiore, although Arabic is dropped after the first two grades. What has been said here applies equally to the *Istituto Tecnico per Geometri*, Mogadiscio.

(vii) The *Arabic and Islamic Institute* conducts post-Intermediate courses through the medium of Arabic in its preparation of teachers and Islamic lawyers; its staff consists at present of eight members from the United Arab Republic and two Somalis. Italian is taught as a subject.

The overall pattern is as follows. Numbers in brackets refer to the study of French or Italian by literary specialists only at the Egyptian Secondary School.

|          | Arabic | English | French | Italian | Russian |
|----------|--------|---------|--------|---------|---------|
| Medium   | 2      | 2       |        | 4       |         |
| Subject  | 5      | 5       | (1)    | 1 (1)   | 1       |

The place of Italian in the various curricula as compared with Arabic and English (used as *medium* and taught as a *subject*) should be noted.

# 12 Generative Linguistics and Socio-linguistics

For Malinowski (1935) the real linguistic fact is the 'full utterance within its context of situation' (p. 11). Side by side with the context of reference 'we have another context: the situation in which the words have been uttered'. The duty of the ethnographer is to put words back where they come from, and the main object of linguistic study is 'living speech in its actual context of situation'; this in turn requires 'the empirical approach to linguistics' rather than one 'largely confined to deductive arguments' (1937, p. 63). Malinowski saw language primarily as a mediator of social purpose. J. R. Firth owed a great deal to Malinowski, and shared this view in all essentials, but at the same time regarded it as an excessively 'realist' approach which over-emphasized the 'brute fact' or 'concrete situation' in which the utterance is 'directly embedded' (J. R. Firth, 1957). Firth wished to bring a sense of order into what seemed to him in danger of becoming an endless series of merely particularistic observations.

Malinowski was fundamentally concerned to uproot the Saussurean distinction between 'langue' (the code of the language maintained in the 'collective conscience' of the speech community) and 'parole' (the manifold realizations of langue in everyday speech and writing). The former, in Malinowski's view (1937), is 'only the general norm' of the latter. That being the case, the linguist's primary objective must be to assist in demonstrating how parole, or human speech activity, is determined or modified by 'contexts of situation'.

A reasonable representation of the opposite view—that of the supposed hopelessness of a direct assault on parole—is given by

J. Berry (1966), in his introduction to a recent edition of the second volume of Malinowski's *The Language of Magic and Gardening*. Berry's main point is that the meaning of an utterance cannot be 'determined' by its context of situation, far less analysed in these terms, since contexts are infinite. Unless some way of reducing such infinite variety can be found, context of situation will have to remain 'below the level of general abstract theory' (xv), hence of no particular interest.

Berry's argument is on a par with that of J. J. Katz and J. A. Fodor (1963), whose illustration of the 'disambiguation' problem inherent in such expressions as 'alligator shoes' and 'horse shoes' is designed to stress the infinite accidents which go into our 'knowledge of the world': that is to say, there may be shoes made from alligators or, conceivably, shoes to fit alligators, but nothing in the make-up of the phrase itself will tell us which sense is appropriate on any given occasion. There *is* something, however, in the make-up of the phrase that gives these two possibilities for interpretation. In other words, for Berry, Katz and Fodor, and for many others, the meaning of an utterance is 'autonomous', context of situation merely providing 'a clue to the particular meaning' with which a word or utterance is used. In this way not only is one of the outer limits of the subject matter of linguistics defined, but so also is the inevitable failure of *any* discipline or combination of disciplines to offer a comprehensive theory for context of situation quite clearly illustrated (J. J. Katz and J. A. Fodor, 1963, p. 489).

The answer to the problem of meaning, for the generative linguist, is certainly not Firth's answer either nor any logical extension of it. Firth felt the necessity for an encompassing set of categories for context of situation, amounting to a kind of broad grid or segmentation of determinants of verbal behaviour: 'What we need are more accurately determined linguistic categories for the principal types of sentences and of usage we employ in our various social roles'. But at least two objections have been made. The first is that Firth gave only very general exemplification of what he meant by context of situation. The second is that no orderly segmentation of linguistically relevant contexts would conceal an underlying behaviouristic philosophy.

On the first score Firth is taken to task, for example, by D. T. Langendoen (1964): 'Firth had not even shown how a linguist can isolate a *single* element of a context of situation' (p. 307–9). But the second objection is surely the more important. K. L. Pike (1954–60) did exemplify contextual categories at some length, yet was still severely criticized by M. Gauthier (1963), to the effect that his examples of verbal/non-verbal patterning (breakfast, a church service, a football match) had been carefully chosen to suit his particular purpose, being by their very nature unduly habitual or ritualized, and so distracting attention from the need to emphasize the creative aspect of language use; tied, that is to say, 'to the surface of things'. As J. P. Thorne (1964) has cogently put it, one's attention has to be turned instead to the power capable of organizing the data in the first place.

In this general connexion, N. Chomsky's very effective review (1959) of B. F. Skinner's *Verbal Behaviour* (1957) is well worth reading. Skinner had taken the position that it is of no use to postulate inherent meanings for the forms of language, since these are unobservable and merely perpetuate 'an outdated doctrine of the expression of ideas', kept alive by a 'sort of patchwork' of undeveloped psychological notions. Before we know where we are 'meaning' will be 'assigned an independent existence'. Skinner's manœuvre is to assume that human verbal behaviour is not species-specific, so allowing, therefore, controlled experiments in which the environment of *animals* are manipulated and responses observed. Thus 'response' types can be related to 'stimulus' types, and conclusions drawn from the causation of *human verbal* behaviour.

Chomsky had a great deal to say on Skinner's line of reasoning, almost all of it securing wide concurrence, including that of many who are not sympathetic to the particular linguistic theory put forward by Chomsky himself. A few of his main observations are: that we have no right to assume that basic underlying aspects of verbal behaviour are not specific to human beings alone, rather quite the contrary; that we 'cannot predict verbal behaviour in terms of the stimuli in the speaker's environment, since we do not know what the current stimuli are until he responds' (p. 553); nor for that matter is it possible to go in the opposite direction, identifying aspects of the environment from utterances, since we will then have to explain both scholarly and intuitive evidence for 'latent learning', whereby the stimulus for action comes from within the organism rather than from some external 'reinforcing' agency; that the contribution made thus by the organism is clearly of great importance, but because of the limited capacity of the human brain can only result from the possession or acquisition of a *finite* set of abilities; that this in turn means that the human being in acquiring the ability to handle the *infinite* variety of language has to infer a finite set of *rules*, 'internalised' as 'grammatical competence' (N. Chomsky, 1965, pp. 3–18), and finally that the analyst in turn has to infer the structure of competence from what he—along with native-speaking informants—*intuitively knows* to be acceptable utterances. Elsewhere Chomsky deals with the question of the justification of descriptions of competence, in terms of 'external validation' procedures—which seek to assess the acceptability of sentences generated by the linguist's rules in the light of native speakers' intuitions (N. Chomsky, 1965, pp. 3–27), and 'internal validation' —in terms of their apparent universality, simplicity, and consistency (N. Chomsky, 1965, pp. 27–47).

The native user's 'competence' then is the concern of the generative linguist, not (except at a later stage) his actual accident-prone socially variable 'performance'. It is important to realize that competence in this sense is not a matter of 'structural grammar unconcerned with "meaning" '. Quite the contrary. The generative linguist's rules are intended to operate upon *semantically* meaningful relationships which constitute what is termed the 'deep structure' of the grammar; so that in internalizing the rules of his language the native learner is learning how to handle part of its meaning. Utterances are intuitively felt to be alike or not alike according to their degree of semantic identity.

The semantic character of underlying grammatical relations has been elaborated by some generative linguists to include specific sets of semantic meanings (or 'semantic markers'), related to the grammar by 'projection rules' (J. J. Katz and J. A. Fodor, 1963; J. J. Katz and P. Postal, 1964). They are conceived of as finite in number, and distributed in various ways among the lexical items in the language. Examples are the oppositions 'animate : inanimate', 'human : non-human', 'mass : count', etc. The motivation for this development has been the need to incorporate rule-governed restrictions on the collocability of lexical items—allowing the production, for example, of 'alligator shoes' but preferably not 'alligator linguistics' and certainly not 'alligator colourless'. The sentence 'colourless green ideas sleep furiously' has in its time generated not a few linguistic poets bent on demonstrating that lexico-grammatical restrictions are too loose to be bound within any set of rules; but for the generative linguist himself this remains a good example of a 'deviant' sentence, hence it is up to him to arrive at just those semantic markers and projection rules that in some sense will best prevent it—and others like it—from happening again.

The semantic marker is an extremely atomistic entity, prompting one to ask where each one comes from in the first place, what its empirical justification might be, and why it should be unreasonable to suppose that their total number is likely to approach infinity. Semantic marker analysis is a form of componential analysis, and it is therefore worth reflecting, with J. Lyons (1963a, p. 80), that componential analysis might satisfactorily locate co-ordinates for kinship systems, yet be unable to do so for most other semantic fields. The attempt to impose a distinctive feature patterning upon the use of words at large seems to pave the way for criticism of the same order as that of C. Lévi-Strauss when, originally in 1945, he dismissed an earlier sociological attempt at a distinctive feature analysis of kinship on the grounds that it was neither realistic, nor simplifying, nor explanatory. 'If system there is', he wrote, 'it could only be conceptual' (1958,

p. 42). Or to put it another way, since lexical items (to greater and to lesser extents) convey social and cultural meaning, then, to that extent, Katz and Fodor are engaging in a kind of micro-sociology (or anthropology) in much of their semantic work, which might well fall far short of what they concede to be the merely 'limited theory of selection by socio-physical setting' (p. 489) within reach of self-confessed socio-linguists.

It is difficult to say how far semantic marker analysis gives priority to method over subject matter, but this is certainly the case in a recent attempt to apply generative linguistic methodology to the characterization of 'pragmatic rules'. The notion of 'pragmatic rules' (which were suggested in passing by G. A. Miller, 1965, as perhaps one day capable of characterizing 'our unlimited variety of belief systems') has been taken up very seriously by O. Werner (1966) and others. Werner defines his pragmatic subject matter as, among other things: 'a psycho-logical analysis of the relation between speaking behaviour and other behaviour; a psychological theory of different connotations of one and the same word for different individuals; ethnological and sociological studies of the speaking habits and their differences in different tribes, different age groups, and social strata' (p. 59). The last part 'includes the "ethnography of speaking" (D. H. Hymes, 1962, 1964a) and socio-linguistics'. In one place Werner states: 'Pragmatics accounts for the ability of native speakers to understand (and use) language in a manner that is culturally appro-priate and results in pragmatically interpreted sentences' (p. 44).

The general field which Werner wishes to stake out is broad and fundamental. Even so, his is a sentence- and word-based theory which owes much to the methods of Katz and Fodor. 'Minimum atomic Plans' take the place of 'semantic markers', and comprise a 'set of active verbs' which cannot be further subdivided 'without difficulty'. The attempt does not work out, its author admitting that the 'cultural competence' he seeks may after all be 'simply lists' (p. 61). M. Durbin (1966), on 'The goals of ethnoscience', in the same volume, reiterates some of the main requirements for a theory of grammatical competence as set out by Chomsky (1965), assuming without further illustration a very closely analogous set of categories for the analysis of 'cultural competence'. Some doubt may be cast therefore not only on the atomistic view of meaning which seems to mark the approach of Katz and Fodor, but also on the assumption that the field of pragmatics—particularly in the sense which Werner attributes to the term—should or even can be handled in a similar manner.

But the more fundamental choice (or denial of choice) between langue and parole has still to be made. The affinity between de Saussure and the generative linguist at this underlying level is very close. Langue and parole are indeed related, as Chomsky (1964a, p. 52) points out, to 'competence' and 'performance' respectively. In emphasizing the former, Chomsky like de Saussure (1931) holds firmly to a mentalist view of language. Thus: 'In evaluating a particular generative grammar, we ask whether the information that it gives us about a language is correct, that is, whether it describes correctly the linguistic intuition of the speaker (de Saussure's "conscience des sujets parlants", which to him, as to Sapir, provides the ultimate test of adequacy for a linguistic description)' (1964a, p. 62). In this particular connection the term 'mentalist' does not imply 'traditional conceptual' notions of 'dualism' ('mind' totally separate from 'body' . . .). But neither in generative nor in Saussurean terms does it reject the *composite* 'sound-image' nature of linguistic units, whether these are phonemes, deep structures, lexical items, or whatever. It is its essentially *relational* nature that preserves de Saussure's 'sign' against a valid imputation of dualism. A sign is a relational composite of 'signifiant' and 'signifié'; the whole sign, not merely the signifiant, constitutes 'form'. The formal structure of a language is expressed, again relationally, in terms of inter-relations ('valeur') among signs; and signs are largely *defined* by such inter-relations ('logical and psychological relations that bind together coexisting terms and form a system in the collective conscience of speakers').

Taken in this general sense, it is very difficult indeed to deny a mentalistic basis to verbal behaviour. But it is equally difficult to turn a blind eye to the vastly significant social and cultural element which it also contains. Taking the two together, it seems profitable to think in terms of some form of 'socio-linguistic competence' the component 'signs' of which need not *necessarily* match those which linguistics may already be more accustomed to handle. J. B. Casagrande (1963, p. 287) quotes some particularly well-chosen words of A. I. Hallowell (1955): '. . . all human cultures must provide the individual with basic orientations that are among the necessary conditions for the development, reinforcement, and effective functioning of self-awareness.' Hallowell himself singles out three such basic orientations: self-other orientation, spatio-temporal orientation, and object orientation, each common to all cultures. It is noticeable that the kind of evidence which supports each one is primarily that of words, grammatical and lexical, Thus, respectively, these include: personal pronoun systems, kinship terms, personal names, terms for psychophysiological processes such as dreaming, listening, etc.; names for places and significant topographical features; and the 'orientation of the self to a phenomenological world of objects'. It is impossible to deny the orientating power of language in respects such as these, yet one can still imagine that in starting out from words rather than from other sorts of linguistic unit Hallowell may very well have excluded or been deflected from orientations of far greater significance and generality. The rest of this account will try to connect with the question of how language enters into and modifies some of the more basic human orientations towards social and cultural environment. Relevant linguistic units are not likely to be exhaustive of *all* the grammar, or all the lexicon, etc., and at the same time must be expected to range in scale from the minutest stylistic variants to distinct languages, and dialects.

In this sense socio-linguistics takes up a very largely mentalistic and non-behaviouristic position, not wholly incompatible with that of generative linguistics, but concerned very much more directly with basic human orientation towards social and cultural environment.

## FURTHER REFERENCES

On grammatical *rules*:

CHOMSKY, N. (1961b). 'Some methodological remarks on generative grammar', in Allen, W. B. *Applied English Linguistics*, 138–41.

FODOR, J. A. and KATZ, J. J. (1963). *The Structure of Language*, 481–2.

MILLER, G. A. (1962b). 'Some psychological theories of grammar', in *American Psychologist*, 754 ff.

MILLER, G. A. (1964). 'The psycholinguists', in *Encounter*, July.

MILLER, G. A. (1965). 'Some preliminaries to psycholinguistics', in *American Psychologist*.

POSTAL, P. (1964). *Constituent Structure*, 8.

On the distinction between 'competence' ('the speaker-hearer's knowledge of his language') and 'performance' ('the natural use of language in concrete situations'), and on generative grammar as theories of competence:

CHOMSKY, N. (1957). *Syntactic Structures*, 48.

CHOMSKY, N. (1958). 'A transformational approach to syntax', in Fodor, J. A. and Katz, J. J., *The Structure of Language*, 240.

CHOMSKY, N. (1961a). 'On the notion "rule of Grammar"', in Fodor, J. A. and Katz, J. J., 120, 121.

CHOMSKY, N. (1964a). *Current Issues in Linguistic Theory*, in Fodor, J. A. and Katz, J. J., 52–60.

KATZ, J. J. and FODOR, J. A. (1963). 'The structure of a semantic theory', in Fodor, J. A. and Katz, J. J., 482–3.

LYONS, J. (1963b). Review of R. M. W. Dixon *What is Language?*, in *Lingua*, 436 ff.

MILLER, G. A. (1964). 'The psycholinguists', in *Encounter*, July, esp. p. 36.

MILLER, G. A. (1965). 'Some preliminaries to psycholinguistics', in *American Psychologist*.

POSTAL, P. (1964). *Constituent Structure*, 90, fn. 83.

STOCKWELL, R. B. (1963). 'The transformational model of generative or predictive grammar', in Garvin, P. L. *Natural Language and the Computer*, 44 ff.

THORNE, J. P. (1964). 'Grammars and machines', in *Transactions of the Philological Society*, 35 ff.

On methodologies for the elicitation of competence:

CHOMSKY, N. (1964b). Comments in Bellugi, U. and Brown, R. *The Acquisition of Language*, 35 ff.—the aim should be to study *comprehension* rather than production, since the input can then be more controllable.

MILLER, G. A. (1962b). 'Some psychological theories of grammar', in *American Psychologist*, 751—gives priority to comprehension over learning and memory.

MILLER, G. A. (1964). 'The psycholinguists', in *Encounter*, July, 32.

On performance:

CHOMSKY, N. (1961a). 'On the notion "Rule of Grammar" ', in Fodor, J. A. and Katz, J. J., 126–7, fn. 16.

CHOMSKY, N. (1965). *Aspects of the Theory of Syntax*, 10–15.

LYONS, J. (1963a). *Structural Semantics*, 33 ff.

LYONS, J. (1963b). Review of R. M. W. Dixon *What is Language?*, in *Lingua*, 440–1.

MILLER, G. A. (1962a). 'Decision units in speech', in IRE *Transactions in Information Theory*, IT–8 Feb. 1962.

MILLER, G. A. (1962b). 'Some psychological theories of grammar', in *American Psychologist*, esp. p. 760.

THORNE, J. P. (1964). 'Grammars and machines', in *Transactions of the Philological Society*, esp. p. 42.

On performance versus competence models int erms of 'empiricist' versus 'rationalist':

CHOMSKY, N. (1965). *Aspects of the Theory of Syntax*, 47–59; esp. on taxonomic (non-generative) linguistics as necessarily empiricist, p. 52 ff.; and on 'the child's discovery of what from a formal point of view is a deep and abstract theory', p. 55–9.

On the 'external' justification of grammars:

BACH, E. (1964). *Introduction to Transformational Linguistics*, 4 ff.

CHOMSKY, N. (1957). *Syntactic Structures*, 13 ff., and Ch. 9 (on the nature of the 'intuition' to which the linguist can rightly appeal, viz. intuition concerning 'linguistic form' or 'grammaticality' rather than 'acceptability' or 'normality').

CHOMSKY, N. (1961a). 'On the notion "Rule of Grammar"', in Fodor, J. A. and Katz, J. J., 129, fn. 25.

CHOMSKY, N. (1961b). 'Some methodological remarks on generative grammar', in Allen, W. B., *Applied English Linguistics*. Disparages the use of objective tests for the elicitation of judgments of grammaticality, in comparison with 'introspective judgments'—see esp. fn. 18.

CHOMSKY, N. (1964a). *Current Issues in Linguistic Theory*, in Fodor, J. A. and Katz, J. J., 79 ff. (on introspective judgement and operational tests).

LEES, R. B. (1964). Comments on a paper in Bellugi, U. and Brown, R., *The Acquisition of Language*, 96 ff. Two issues: how to elicit judgments of grammaticality from the infant; and evaluation does not measure 'which grammar converges on the *data* faster'.

LEVIN, S. (1962). 'Poetry and grammaticalness', in *Proceedings of the IX International Congress of Linguists*, esp. the concluding section which discusses the problem of the significance of introspective judgments.

LYONS, J. (1963a). *Structural Semantics*, 20 ff. (esp. on the 'limits of grammatical description').

LYONS, J. (1963b). Review of R. M. W. Dixon, *What is Language?*, in *Lingua*, 439 ff.

MACLAY, H. and SLEATOR, M. D. (1960). 'Responses to language: judgments of grammaticalness', in *International Journal of American Linguistics*.

THORNE, J. P. (1964). 'Grammars and machines', in *Transactions of the Philological Society*, 34 ff.

On the 'internal' justification of grammar:

CHOMSKY, N. (1964a). *Current Issues in Linguistic Theory*, in Fodor, J. A. and Katz, J. J., 61 ff.

HALLE, M. (1962). 'Phonology in generative grammar', in Fodor, J. A. and Katz, J. J.

HALLE, M. (1964). 'On the bases of phonology', in Fodor, J. A. and Katz, J. J.

On 'simplicity' as a criterion:

CHOMSKY, N. (1965). *Aspects of the Theory of Syntax*, 37 ff.

8

On the need to discover linguistic universals ('deep underlying similarities among languages'):

CHOMSKY, N. (1964a). *Current Issues in Linguistic Theory*, in Fodor, J. A. and Katz, J. J., 61–79, esp. pp. 61–68. To the extent that a description of the grammar of a language rests upon linguistic universals, so it achieves 'explanatory adequacy': it has 'explained' aspects of the universal human ability to acquire linguistic competence.

CHOMSKY, N. (1965). *Aspects of the Theory of Syntax*, 15–37.

On semantic considerations:

CHOMSKY, N. (1957). *Syntactic Structures*.

CHOMSKY, N. (1964a). *Current Issues in Linguistic Theory*, in Fodor, J. A. and Katz, J. J., 77: 'In general as description becomes deeper, what appear to be semantic questions fall increasingly within its scope.'

CHOMSKY, N. (1965). *Aspects of the Theory of Syntax*, 99, 132 ff., 141 ff.

# BIBLIOGRAPHY

ABERCROMBIE, D. (1956). *Problems and Principles*. Longmans.

ALBERT, E. M. (1964). 'Rhetoric, logic, and poetics in Burundi: culture patterning of speech behaviour', in *American Anthropologist*, 66, 6, 2.

ALLPORT, G. W. (1963). *Pattern and Growth in Personality*. Holt.

ANDRZEJEWSKI, B. W. (1962). 'Speech and writing dichotomy as the pattern of multilingualism in the Somali Republic', in *Symposium on Multilingualism*, Brazzaville, CCTA Publications Bureau, London.

ANDRZEJEWSKI, B. W. (1965). 'Emotional bias in the translation and presentation of African oral art', in *Sierra Leone Language Review*, no. 4.

ANDRZEJEWSKI, B. W. (1967). 'The art of the miniature in Somali poetry', in *African Language Review*, vol. 6.

ANDRZEJEWSKI, B. W. and GALAAL, MUSA H. I. (1966). 'The art of the verbal message in Somali society', in *Neue Afrikanistische Studien*. Hamburg.

Anthropological Linguistics 8, 8 (Nov. 1966). *Ethnoscience.*

ARGYLE, M. (1967). *The Psychology of Interpersonal Behaviour*. Penguin Books.

BACH, E. (1964). *Introduction to Transformational Linguistics*. Holt, Rinehart, Winston.

BARBER, C. (1962). 'Some measurable characteristics of scientific prose'.

BARTH, F. (1966). *Models of Social Organization*. Occasional Paper No. 23, Royal Anthropological Institute of Great Britain and Ireland.

BELLUGI, U. and BROWN, R. (1964). *The Acquisition of Language* (*Monographs of the Society for Research in Child Development*).

BERNSTEIN, B. (1960). 'Language and social class', in *British Journal of Sociology*, 11, 271–6.

BERNSTEIN, B. (1961a). 'Social class and linguistic development: a theory of social learning', in *Society, Economy and Education*, eds. Floud, J., Halsey, A. H. and Anderson, A. The Free Press: Glencoe, Illinois.

BERNSTEIN, B. (1961b). 'Social structure, language and learning', in *Educational Research*, 3, 3, p. 163–76.

BERNSTEIN, B. (1961c). 'Aspects of language in the social process', in Hymes, D. H. (1964c), 251–64; and in *Journal of Child Psychology and Psychiatry*, 1961.

BERNSTEIN, B. (1962). 'Linguistic codes, hesitation phenomena and intelligence', in *Language and Speech*, 5, 1, 31–48.

BERNSTEIN, B. (1964). 'Social class, speech systems and psychotherapy', in *British Journal of Sociology*, 15, 1, 64.

BERNSTEIN, B. (1965). 'A socio-linguistic approach to social learning', in *Penguin Survey of the Social Sciences 1965*.

BERNSTEIN, B. (1966). 'Elaborated and restricted codes', in *Sociological Inquiry*, Spring number entitled *Explorations in Socio-linguistics*.

BERRY, J. (1962). 'Pidgins and creoles in Africa', in *Symposium on Multilingualism*, Brazzaville.

BERRY, J. (1966). Introduction to B. Malinowski, *The Language of Magic and Gardening*. Allen & Unwin.

BLOM, J.-P. and GUMPERZ, J. J. (1967). 'Some social determinants of verbal behaviour.' Unpublished paper presented at the annual general meeting of the American Sociological Association, 1966.

BLOOMFIELD, L. (1933). *Language*. New York: Holt.

BOAS, F. (1911). 'Linguistics and ethnology', in *Handbook of American Indian Languages*, Part I; and in Hymes (1964c), 15–27.

BOOMER, D. S. (1964). 'Linguistics and speech behaviour', in *Monographs on Languages and Linguistics*. Georgetown.

BRADDOCK, R. *et al.* (1963). *Research on Written Composition*. NCTE Champaign, Illinois.

BRIGHT, W. and RAMANUJAN, A. K. (1962). 'Socio-linguistic variation and language change', in *Proceedings of the IX International Congress of Linguists*.

British Council (1960–61). Annual Report. HMSO.

BRITTON, J. N. (1965). 'Speech in the school', in *Some Aspects of Oracy*. National Association for the Teaching of English, Bulletin vol. 2, no. 2.

BROADBENT, D. E. (1967). 'Notes on current knowledge concerning the psychology of modern languages.' Mimeographed CRDML.

BROOK, G. L. (1964). *English Dialects*. Andre Deutsch.

BROSNAHAN, L. F. (1963). 'Some historical cases of language imposition', in Spencer, J., ed. *Language in Africa*. Cambridge University Press.

BROWN, R. and FORD, M. (1961). 'Address in American English', in Hymes (1964c), 234–45; and in *Journal of Abnormal and Social Psychology*, 1961.

BROWN, R. and GILMAN, A. (1960). 'The pronouns of power and solidarity', in *Style in Language*, ed. Sebeok, T. A. London: Wiley.

BRUNER, J. S. (1960). *The Process of Education*. OUP.

BRUNER, J. S. (1962). *On Knowing: Essays for the Left Hand*. Harvard University Press.

BULL, W. E. (1955). 'The use of vernacular languages in fundamental education', in *International Journal of American Linguistics*; and in Hymes (1964c), 527–34.

'Bulletin Signaletique'. Section on 'Sociology of language', in *Language Sciences*. Paris: Centre Nationale de la Recherche Scientifique. Quarterly.

BURNS, T. (1957). 'Management in action', in *Operational Research Quarterly*, 8, 2, p. 45–60.

CARROLL, J. B. (1962). 'Research problems concerning the teaching of foreign or second languages to younger children', in *Foreign Languages in Primary Education*. Unesco Institute for Education, Hamburg. Also OUP (1967).

CARROLL, J. B. and CASAGRANDE, J. B. (1958). 'The function of language classifications in behaviour', in Maccoby (*et al.*), *Readings in Social Psychology*. Holt, Rinehart & Winston.

CASAGRANDE, J. B. (1963). 'Language universals and anthropology', in *Universals of Language*, ed. Greenberg, J. H. MIT Press.

CATFORD, J. C. (1965). *A Linguistic Theory of Translation*. OUP.

CHOMSKY, N. (1957). *Syntactic Structures*. The Hague: Mouton.

CHOMSKY, N. (1958). 'A transformational approach to syntax', in Fodor, J. A. and Katz, J. J. (below).

CHOMSKY, N. (1959). Review of B. F. Skinner *Verbal Behaviour*, in *Language*, 35, 1; and in Fodor, J. A. and Katz, J. J.

CHOMSKY, N. (1961a). 'On the notion "Rule of Grammar" ', in Fodor, J. A. and Katz, J. J.

CHOMSKY, N. (1961b). 'Some methodological remarks on generative grammar', in (*a*) *Word*, 1961, (*b*) Allen, W. B. *Applied English Linguistics*.

CHOMSKY, N. (1962). Discussion following paper in *Proceedings of the IX International Congress of Linguists*.

CHOMSKY, N. (1964a). *Current Issues in Linguistic Theory*. Mouton. Also in Fodor, J. A. and Katz, J. J., and (an earlier version) in *Proceedings of the IX International Congress of Linguists*.

CHOMSKY, N. (1964b). Comments in Bellugi, U. and Brown, R., *The Acquisition of Language*.

CHOMSKY, N. (1965). *Aspects of the Theory of Syntax*. MIT.

CHOMSKY, N. (1966). 'Linguistic Theory', in *Northeast Conference on the Teaching of Foreign Languages*.

CHRISTOPHERSEN, P. (1960). 'Towards a standard of International English', in *English Language Teaching*, 14, 3.

COHEN, M. (1956). *Pour une Sociologie du langage*. Paris: Albin Michel.

DE SAUSSURE, F. (1931). *Course in General Linguistics*, ed. Bally, C. and Sechehaye, A., and translated by Baskin, W. London, 1961.

DEUTSCH, K. W. (1953). *Nationalism and Social Communication*. New York: John Wiley & Sons.

DIEBOLD, A. R. (1961). 'Incipient bilingualism', in *Language*, 97–112; and in Hymes (1964c), 495–511.

DIEBOLD, A. R. (1962). 'Mexican and Guatemalan Bilingualism', in *Study of the Role of Second Languages*, ed. Rice, F. A. Center for Applied Linguistics, Washington, D.C.

DIEBOLD, A. R. (1964). Review of Sol Saporta, *Psycholinguistics*, in *Language*, vol. 40, no. 2, 197–260.

DURBIN, M. (1966). 'The goals of ethnoscience', in *Anthropological Linguistics*, 8, 8 (November).

ELLIS, J. (1966a). 'On contextual meaning', in *In Memory of J. R. Firth*. Longmans, Green & Co.

ELLIS, J. (1966b). *Towards a General Comparative Linguistics*. Mouton.

ERVIN-TRIPP, S. (1964). 'An analysis of the interaction of language, topic and listener', in *American Anthropologist*, 66, 6, 2.

EVANS-PRITCHARD, E. E. (1956). 'Sanza, a characteristic feature of Zande language and thought', in *Bulletin of the School of Oriental and African Studies*, vol. 18.

EVANS-PRITCHARD, E. E. (1963). 'Meaning in Zande proverbs', in *Man*.

EVANS-PRITCHARD, E. E. (1964). 'Zande proverbs: final selection and comments', in *Man*.

The Examining of English Language (1964). Eighth Report of the Secondary School Examinations Council. London: HMSO.

FEARING, F. (1964). 'Human communication', in *People, Society and Mass Communications*, ed. Dexter, L. A. and White, D. M.

FERGUSON, C. A. (1959). 'Diglossia', in *Word*, 15, 325–40, and in Hymes (1964c), 429–40.

FERGUSON, C. A. (1962a). 'Background to second language problems', in *Study of the Role of Second Languages*, ed. Rice, F. A.

FERGUSON, C. A. (1962b). 'Principles of teaching languages with diglossia', in *Monograph Series on Languages and Linguistics*. Georgetown University, no. 15.

FIRTH, J. R. (1935). 'The techniques of semantics', in *Transactions of the Philological Society*, and in *Papers in Linguistics 1934–1951*. OUP.

FIRTH, J. R. (1937). *The Tongues of Men*. Watts & Co. (Also OUP, 1964.)

FIRTH, J. R. (1957). 'Ethnographic analysis and language', in *Man and Culture*, ed. Firth, R. Routledge & Kegan Paul.

FISCHER, J. L. (1958). 'Social influence in the choice of a linguistic variant', in *Word*; also in Allen, H. B., *Readings in Applied English Linguistics*; also in Hymes (1964c).

FISHMAN, J. A. (1965). 'Who speaks what language to whom and when?', in *La Linguistique*.

FISHMAN, J. A. (1966). *Language Loyalty in the United States*. Mouton.

FISHMAN, J. A. (1967). 'Bilingualism with and without diglossia; diglossia with and without bilingualism', in *Journal of Social Issues*, vol. 23, no. 2.

FODOR, J. A. and KATZ, J. J. (1963). *The Structure of Language*. Prentice-Hall.

FRAKE, C. O. (1962). 'Cultural ecology and ethnography', in *American Anthropologist*, 64.

FRASER, G. S. (1965). 'How students write', *Times Literary Supplement*, 14 January.

FRIEDRICH, P. (1966). 'The structural implications of Russian pronominal usage', in Bright, W. (1966).

GARDNER, R. C. (1966). 'Motivational variables in second-language learning', in *Language Learning: the Individual and the Process*, IJAL, 32, 1.

GARVIN, P. L. (1959). 'The standard language problem: concepts and methods', in *Anthropological Linguistics*, 1, 2; and in Hymes, D. (1964c).

GARVIN, P. L. and MATHIOT, M. (1960). 'The urbanisation of the Guarani language', in Wallace, A. F. C., ed. *Men and Cultures: Selected Papers of the Fifth International Congress of Anthropological and Ethnological Sciences*. University of Pennsylvania Press.

GAUTHIER, M. (1963). Review of K. L. Pike (1954–60), in *Word*.

GEERTZ, C. (1960). *The Religion of Java*. Glencoe: Free Press.

GOODALL, R. J. (1964). 'An ethnolinguistic bibliography with supporting material in linguistics and anthropology', in *Anthropological Linguistics*, 6, 2.

GOODENOUGH, W. H. (1961). 'Education and identity', in *Anthropology and Education*, ed. Gruber, F. C.

GOODENOUGH, W. H. (1965). 'Rethinking status and role', in *The Relevance of Models for Social Anthropology*. Tavistock Publications.

GREGORY, M. (1967). 'Aspects of varieties differentiation', in *Journal of Linguistics*.

GUMPERZ, J. J. (1961). 'Speech variation and the study of Indian civilisation', in *American Anthropologist*; and in Hymes (1964c).

GUMPERZ, J. J. (1962a). 'Hindi-Punjabi code-switching in Delhi', in *Proceedings of the IX International Congress of Linguists*.

GUMPERZ, J. J. (1962b). 'Types of linguistic communities', in *Anthropological Linguistics*, 4, 1.

GUMPERZ, J. J. (1962c). 'Language problems in the rural development of North India', in *Study of the Role of Second Languages*, ed. Rice, F. A.

GUMPERZ, J. J. (1964). 'Linguistic and social interaction in two communities', in *American Anthropologist*, 66, 6, 2.

GUMPERZ, J. J. (1965a). 'Linguistic repertoires, grammars and second language instructions', in *Monograph Series on Language and Linguistics*. Georgetown University, No. 18.

GUMPERZ, J. J. (1965b). 'Language', in *Biennial Review of Anthropology*, ed. Siegel, B. J. Stanford University Press.

GUMPERZ, J. J. (1966). 'On the ethnology of linguistic change', in Bright, W. (1966).

GUMPERZ, J. J. (1967a). 'On the linguistic markers of bilingual communication', in *Journal of Social Issues*, vol. 23, no. 2.

GUMPERZ, J. J. (1967b). 'How can we describe and measure the behaviour of bilingual groups', in *Conference on Bilingualism*. Moncton.

GUMPERZ, J. J. and NAIM, C. M. (1960). 'Formal and informal standards in the Hindi language area', in Ferguson, C. A. and Gumperz, J. J. (1960).

HAAS, M. R. (1944). 'Men's and women's speech in Koasati', in *Language*; also in Hymes (1964c).

HALL, R. A. JR. (1965). Article in *Foundations of Language*.

HALL, R. A. (1966). *Pidgin and Creole Languages*. Cornell University Press.

HALLE, M. (1962). 'Phonology in generative grammar', in Fodor, J. A. and Katz, J. J.; also in *Word*.

HALLE, M. (1964). 'On the bases of phonology', in Fodor, J. A. and Katz, J. J.

HALLIDAY, M. A. K. (1961). 'Categories of the theory of grammar', in *Word*.

HALLIDAY, M. A. K., McINTOSH, A. and STREVENS, P. D. (1964). *The Linguistic Sciences and Language Teaching*. Longmans.

HALLOWELL, A. I. (1955). *Culture and Experience*. Philadelphia.

HAUGEN, E. (1953). *The Norwegian Language in America: A Study in Bilingual Behaviour*. Philadelphia: University of Pennsylvania Press. 2 vols.

HAUGEN, E. (1956). *Bilingualism in the Americas: A Bibliography and Research Guide*. American Dialect Society.

HAUGEN, E. (1959). 'Planning for a standard language in modern Norway', in *Anthropological Linguistics*, 1, 3.

HAUGEN, E. (1962). 'Schizoglossia and the linguistic norm', in *Monograph Series on Languages and Linguistics*. Georgetown University, no. 15.

HAUGEN, E. (1966a) 'Language, dialect, nation', in *American Anthropologist*, 68, 4.

HAUGEN, E. (1966b). 'Linguistics and language planning', in Bright, W. (1966).

HAUGEN, E. (1966c). *Language Conflict and Language Planning*. Harvard University Press.

HAYES, A. S. (1964). 'Paralinguistics and kinesics: pedagogical perspectives', in *Approaches to Semiotics*, ed. Sebeok, T. A. Mouton.

HERTZLER, J. O. (1965). *A Sociology of Language*. Random House.

HILL, A. A. (1958). 'Prescriptivism and linguistics in English teaching', in Allen, H. B., *Readings in Applied English Linguistics*.

HOENIGSWALD, H. M. (1962). 'Bilingualism, presumable bilingualism, and diachrony', in *Anthropological Linguistics*, vol. 4, no. 1.

HOENIGSWALD, H. M. (1966). 'A proposal for the study of folk-linguistics', in Bright, W. (1966).

HOIJER, H. (1961). 'Anthropological linguistics', in *Trends in European and American Linguistics, 1936–1960*. Utrecht and Antwerp: Spectrum.

HOPE, T. E. (1962–3). 'Loan-words as cultural and lexical symbols', in *Archivum Linguisticum*, 14, 2; 15, 1.

HOUSEHOLDER, F. W. (1962). 'Greek diglossia', in *Monograph Series on Languages and Linguistics*. Georgetown University, no. 15.

HYMES, D. H. (1961a). 'Linguistic aspects of cross-cultural personality study', in *Studying Personality Cross-Culturally*, ed. Kaplan, B. Harper & Row.

HYMES, D. H. (1961b). 'Functions of speech: an evolutionary approach', in *Anthropology and Education*, ed. Gruber, F. C. Philadelphia: University of Pennsylvania Press.

HYMES, D. H. (1962). 'The ethnography of speaking', in Gladwin, T. and Sturtevant, W. C. (eds.) *Anthropology and Human Behaviour*. Washington, D.C.: Anthropological Society of Washington.

HYMES, D. H. (1963). 'Towards a history of linguistic anthropology', in *Anthropological Linguistics*, 5, 1.

HYMES, D. H. (1964a). 'Toward ethnographies of communication', in *American Anthropologist*, 66, 6, 2.

HYMES, D. H. (1964b). 'Directions in (ethno-) linguistic theory', in *American Anthropologist*, 66, 3, 2.

HYMES, D. H. (1964c). *Language in Culture and Society: A Reader in Linguistics and Anthropology*. Harper & Row.

HYMES, D. H. (1964d). Comments on a paper by Bullowa, M., in Bellugi, U. and Brown, R. (1964).

IJAL. = *International Journal of American Linguistics*.

INKELES, A. (1966). 'Social structure and the socialization of competence', in *Harvard Educational Review*, 36, 3.

International Bibliography of Social and Cultural Anthropology. London: Stevens & Sons Ltd.

International Bibliography of Sociology. London: Stevens & Sons Ltd.

JAKOBSON, R. (1960). 'Linguistics and poetics', in *Style in Language*, ed. Sebeok, T. A. New York: Wiley.

JOOS, M. (1962). *The Five Clocks*. Mouton.

KATZ, J. J. and FODOR, J. A. (1963). 'The structure of a semantic theory', in *Language*; also in *The Structure of Language*, ed. Fodor, J. A. and Katz, J. J.

KATZ, J. J. and POSTAL, P. (1964). *An Integrated Theory of Linguistic Descriptions*. The MIT Press.

KENYON, J. S. (1948). 'Cultural levels and functional varieties of English', in Allen, H. B. *Readings in Applied English Linguistics*.

KLEIN, J. (1965). *Samples from English Culture*. Routledge & Kegan Paul.

KLOSS, H. (1966). 'Types of multilingual communities: a discussion of ten variables', in *Sociological Inquiry*, Spring.

LABOV, W. (1963). 'The social motivation of a sound change', in *Word*.

LABOV, W. (1964). 'Phonological correlates of social stratification', in *American Anthropologist*, 66, 2.

LABOV, W. (1965). 'Stages in the acquisition of standard English', in Shuy, R. W. (1965).

LABOV, W. (1966a). 'The effect of social mobility on linguistic behaviour', in *Sociological Inquiry*, Spring.

LABOV, W. (1966b). *The Social Stratification of English in New York City.* Center for Applied Linguistics.

LAMBERT, W. E. *et al.* (1961). *A Study of the Roles of Attitudes and Motivation in Second Language Learning.* Mimeographed.

LAMBERT, W. W. and LAMBERT, W. E. (1964). *Social Psychology.* Prentice-Hall.

LAMBERT, W. E. (1967). 'A social psychology of bilingualism', in *Journal of Social Issues*, vol. 23, no. 2.

LANGENDOEN, D. T. (1964). Review of *Studies in Linguistic Analysis*, in *Language*, 40, 2.

LASHLEY, K. S. (1951). 'The problem of serial order in behaviour', in *Psycholinguistics*, ed. Saporta, Sol (1963).

LAWTON, D. (1963). 'Social class differences in language development', in *Language and Speech*, 6, 3.

LAWTON, D. (1964). 'Social class language difference in group discussions', in *Language and Speech*, 7, 3.

LE PAGE, R. B. (1964). *The National Language Question.* OUP.

LEE, D. (1961). 'Autonomous motivation', in *Anthropology and Education*, ed. Gruber, F. C.

LEES, R. B. (1958a). 'Transformational grammars and the fries framework', in Allen, W. B. *Applied English Linguistics.*

LEES, R. B. (1958b). 'Some neglected aspects of parsing,' in Allen, W. B.

LEES, R. B. (1964). Comments on a paper in Bellugi, U. and Brown, R. (1964).

LENNEBERG, E. H. (1953). 'Cognition in ethnolinguistics', in *Language*.

LENNEBERG, E. H. (1962). 'The relationship of language to formation of concepts', in *Synthese*, 14.

LEVIN, S. (1962). 'Poetry and grammaticalness', in *Proceedings of the IX International Congress of Linguists*.

Linguistic Bibliography. Permanent International Committee of Linguists. Utrecht: Spectrum.

Linguistic Reporter. Newsletter of the Center for Applied Linguistics, 1717 Massachusetts Avenue, N.W. Washington, D.C. 20036.

LOUNSBURY, F. (1959, 1962). 'Language', in Siegel, B. J. (ed.) *Biennial Review of Anthropology*. Stanford University Press.

LYONS, J. (1963a). *Structural Semantics*. Blackwell.

LYONS, J. (1963b). Review of R. M. W. Dixon (above) in *Lingua*.

LYONS, J. and WALES, R. J. (1966), eds. *Psycholinguistics Papers*. Edinburgh University Press.

MACLAY, H. and SLEATOR, M. D. (1960). 'Responses to language: judgments of grammaticalness', in *International Journal of American Linguistics*.

MALINOWSKI, B. (1923). 'The problem of meaning in primitive languages', in Ogden, C. K. and Richards, I. A. *The Meaning of Meaning*. Kegan Paul.

MALINOWSKI, B. (1935). *Coral Gardens and their Magic*, vol. II. London: Allen & Unwin.

MALINOWSKI, B. (1937). 'The dilemma of contemporary linguistics', in Hymes (1964c).

MARCKWARDT, A. H. and QUIRK, R. (1964). *A Common Language*. BBC Publications.

MARTIN, S. E. (1964). 'Speech levels in Japan and Korea', in Hymes (1964c).

MBAGA, K. and WHITELEY, W. H. (1961). 'Formality and informality in Yao speech', in *Africa*, 31, 2.

McINTOSH, A. (1963). 'Language and style', in *Durham University Journal*.

McINTOSH, A. (1965). 'Saying', in *Review of English Literature*, vol. 6, no. 2.

MILLER, G. A. (1956). 'The magical number seven, plus or minus two: some limits on our capacity for processing information', in *The Psychological Review*, 63.

MILLER, G. A. (1951). *Language and Communication*. McGraw-Hill Book Co.

MILLER, G. A. (1962a). 'Decision units in speech', in IRE *Transactions in Information Theory*, IT–8 February 1962.

MILLER, G. A. (1962b). 'Some psychological theories of grammar', in *American Psychologist*.

MILLER, G. A. (1964). 'The psycholinguists', in *Encounter*, July.

MILLER, G. A. (1965). 'Some preliminaries to psycholinguistics', in *American Psychologist*.

MILLER, G. A., GALANTER, E. and PRIBRAM, R. (1960). *Plans and the Structure of Behaviour*. New York: Holt.

MITCHELL, T. F. (1965). *On the Nature of Linguistics and its Place in University Studies*. Leeds University Press.

McQUOWN, N. A. (1962). 'Indian and Ladino bilingualism: socio-cultural contrasts in Chiapas, Mexico', in *Monograph Series on Language and Linguistics*. Georgetown University, no. 15.

MOHRMANN, C. *et al.* (1961). *Trends in European and American Linguistics 1930–1960*. Utrecht and Antwerp: Spectrum.

MOULTON, W. G. (1962). 'What standard for diglossia? The case of German Switzerland', in *Monograph Series on Language and Linguistics*. Georgetown University, no. 15.

NEWMAN, S. (1964). 'Vocabulary levels: Zuni sacred and slang usage', in Hymes (1964c).

The Newsom Report ('Half our future'). A report of the Central Advisory Council for Education. HMSO (1963).

OSGOOD, C. (1963). 'Language universals and psycholinguistics', in *Universals of Language*, ed. Greenberg, J. H.

PERREN, G. E. (1959a, 1959b, 1960). 'Training and research in English teaching: the work of the special centre in Nairobi', in *Overseas Education*, vol. 31.

PERREN, G. E. and HOLLOWAY, M. F. (1965). *Language and Communication in the Commonwealth*. HMSO.

PIA, J. J. (1966). 'Language in Somalia', in *Linguistic Reporter*, 8, 3.

PIKE, K. L. (1954–60). *Language in Relation to a Unified Theory of Human Behaviour*, Parts 1–3. Glendale, California, Summer Institute of Linguistics.

PIKE, K. L. (1967). As (1954–60), new edition. Mouton.

POSTAL, P. (1964). *Constituent Structure*. Mouton.

PRIDE, J. B. (1963). 'Beginnings and endings', Dissertation, Department of Applied Linguistics, University of Edinburgh.

PRIDE, J. B. (1968). 'Analysing classroom procedures', in *Applied Linguistics and the Teaching of English*. Longmans.

QUIRK, R. (1962). *The English we Use*. Longmans.

RAY, P. S. (1963). *Language Standardisation*. The Hague: Mouton.

ROBINSON, W. P. (1965a). 'Cloze procedure as a technique for the investigation of social class differences in language usage', in *Language and Speech*, 8, 1.

ROBINSON, W. P. (1965b). 'The elaborated code in working class language', in *Language and Speech*, 8, 2.

RUBIN, J. (1962). 'Bilingualism in Paraguay', in *Anthropological Linguistics*, 4, 1.

SALISBURY, R. F. (1962). 'Notes on bilingualism and linguistic change in New Guinea', in *Anthropological Linguistics*, vol. 4, no. 7.

SAMARIN, W. J. (1966). 'Self-annulling prestige factors among speakers of a Creole language', in Bright, W. (1966).

SAPIR, E. (1921). *Language*. New York: Harcourt, Brace.

SAPIR, E. (1924). 'The grammarian and his language', in *Selected Writings of Edward Sapir*, ed. Mandelbaum, D. G. Berkeley & Los Angeles, University of California Press (1949).

SAPIR, E. (1929). 'The status of linguistics as a science', in Mandelbaum, D. G.

SAPIR, E. (1931a). 'Communication', in Mandelbaum, D. G.

SAPIR, E. (1931b). 'Dialect', in Mandelbaum, D. G.

SAPIR, E. (1933). 'Language', in Mandelbaum, D. G.

SCHATZMAN, L. and STRAUSS, A. (1955). 'Social class and modes of communication', in *American Journal of Sociology*.

SCUPHAM, J. (1966). 'The social factor in education', in *The Advancement of Science*, 23, 111.

SHUY, R. W. ed. (1965). *Social Dialects and Language Learning*. NCTE, Champaign, Illinois.

SILVERMAN, S. (1966). 'An ethnographic approach to social stratification: prestige in a central Indian community', in *American Anthropologist*, 68, 4.

SKINNER, B. F. (1957). *Verbal Behaviour*. Appleton-Century-Crofts, Inc.

SMALL, J. (1964). 'Illiteracy in high places', in *Times Educational Supplement*.

SMITH, F. and MILLER, G. A. (1965). *The Genesis of Language*. Cambridge, Mass.

'Somalia' (1965). Advisory Mission on Development of Higher Education. UNESCO.

SPENCE, N. C. W. (1964). 'The basic problems in ethnolinguistics', in *Archivum Linguisticum*.

Sprott, W. J. H. (1958). *Human Groups*. Penguin.

Stankiewicz, E. (1964). 'Problems of emotive language', in *Approaches to Semiotics*, ed. Sebeok, T. A.

Stern, H. H. (1962). *Foreign Languages in Primary Education*. UNESCO Institute for Education, Hamburg. See also the OUP edition (1967).

Stewart, W. A. (1962a). 'An outline of linguistic typology for describing multilingualism', in *Study of the Role of Second Languages*, ed. Rice.

Stewart, W. A. (1962b). 'Creole languages in the Caribbean', in *Study of the Role of Second Languages*, ed. Rice, F. A. Center for Applied Linguistics, Washington, D.C.

Stewart, W. A. (1962c). 'The functional distribution of Creole and French in Haiti', in *Monograph Series on Languages and Linguistics*. Georgetown University, No. 13.

Stewart, W. A. ed. (1964). *Non-standard Speech and the Teaching of English*. Language Information Series 2. Center for Applied Linguistics.

Stewart, W. A. (1965). 'Urban Negro speech: sociolinguistic factors affecting English teaching', in Shuy, R. W. (1965).

Stockwell, R. B. (1963). 'The transformational model of generative or predictive grammar', in Garvin, P. L. *Natural Language and the Computer*. McGraw-Hill.

Tanner, N. (1967). 'Speech and society among the Indonesian elite: a case study of a multilingual society', in *Anthropological Linguistics*, 9, 3.

Thorne, J. P. (1964). 'Grammars and machines', in *Transactions of the Philological Society*.

Trim, J. L. M. (1961). 'English standard pronunciation', in *English Language Teaching*, 16, 1.

Ullmann, S. (1962). *Semantics*. Oxford: Blackwell.

UNESCO (1953). *The Use of Vernacular Languages in Education*. (Monographs on Fundamental Education, No. 8.) Paris: UNESCO.

Vickers, G. (1955). 'Communication in economic systems', in *Studies in Communication*. London.

Vildomec, V. (1963). *Multilingualism*. Sythoff-Leyden, A. W.

Walsh, W. (1964). *A Human Idiom*. London: Chatto & Windus.

Weinreich, U. (1953). *Languages in Contact*. Mouton.

Weinreich, U. (1957). 'Functional aspects of Indian bilingualism', in *Word*.

Weinreich, U. (1958). 'Research frontiers in bilingualism studies', in *Proceedings of the Eighth International Congress of Linguists*.

WEINREICH, U. (1963). 'On the semantic structure of language', in *Universals of Language*, ed. Greenberg, J. H.

WERNER, O. (1956). 'Pragmatics and ethnoscience', in *Anthropological Linguistics*, 8, 8.

WHITELEY, W. H. (1966). 'Social anthropology, meaning and linguistics', in *Man*, 1, 2.

WHITELEY, W. H. (1967). 'Loanwords in linguistic description: a case study from Tanzania, East Africa', in *Approaches in Linguistic Methodology*, ed. Rauch, I. and Scott, C. T.

WHORF, B. L. Esp. 'A linguistic consideration of thinking in primitive communities', 'Some verbal categories of Hopi', 'The relation of habitual thought and behaviour to language', 'Language, mind, and reality', in *Language, Thought and Reality*, ed. Carroll, J. B.

WOLFF, H. (1959). 'Intelligibility and inter-ethnic attitudes', in *Anthropological Linguistics*. Also in Hymes (1964c).

YOUNG, J. Z. (1955). 'The influence of language on medicine', in *Studies in Communication*. London.

KING ALFRED'S COLLEGE
LIBRARY